THE MOBIUS GUIDES
angels

THE MOBIUS GUIDES

angels

LYNN PALMER

HODDER
MOBIUS

Copyright © 1999, 2003 by Lynn Palmer

First published in Great Britain in 2003 by Hodder and Stoughton
A division of Hodder Headline

The right of Lynn Palmer to be identified as the Author
of the Work has been asserted by her in accordance with the
Copyright, Designs and Patents Act 1988.

A Mobius paperback

1 3 5 7 9 10 8 6 4 2

All rights reserved. No part of this publication may be reproduced, stored
in a retrieval system, or transmitted, in any form or by any means without
the prior written permission of the publisher, nor be otherwise circulated
in any form of binding or cover other than that in which it is published
and without a similar condition being imposed on the subsequent
purchaser.

A CIP catalogue record for this title is
available from the British Library

ISBN 0 34073474 4

Typeset in Fairfield Light by
Palimpsest Book Production Limited, Polmont, Stirlingshire
Printed and bound in Great Britain by
Mackays of Chatham Ltd, Chatham, Kent

Hodder and Stoughton
A division of Hodder Headline
338 Euston Road
London NW1 3BH

With my love this book is dedicated to Guy and Claire.
The gift of a child is beyond measure.

acknowledgements

Love and thanks to Teresa, Kathleen and Tony, for encouragement, support and IT.

contents

Part 1: About Angels   1

1 introduction to angels   3

Positive loving thoughts cast light   4
The background   6
The book   7
The history   8
The practical   9

2 what is an angel?   10

A soldier's angel – voices   10
Fragrance   12
Dreams   13
Angel of mine – A beautiful creature   14
Protection   16

3 image of angels   18

Philosophers   19
Religion   19
Primitive   22
Modern   23

Part 2: Angelology 25

4 tree of the angelic world 28

First Triad 29
Second Triad 30
Third Triad 31
Origins of Angelology 34
Special functions 38

5 knowledge of angels 41

Michael – Prince of Light 41
Gabriel – Angel of Humanity 42
Raphael – Divine Physician 43
Uriel – Angel of Repentance 44
Metatron – Angel of the Lord 45
Sandalphon – Guardian Spirit 46
Samuel – Angel of Evil 46
The feminine principle 47
Sophia – Angel of Wisdom 48
Israfil – Angel of Judgment Day 48

Part 3: Working with Angels 51

6 angel calling cards 53

Asking 54
Intuition 56
The cards 57
The words 57
The place 58
Motivation 59
Inventory 60
Relaxation 61

Meditation	62
Contact	62
Recap of centring	64

7 help for ourselves — 66

Angel therapy – How does it work?	66
Energy	68
Etheric exercise	69
Healing properties	71
Colours	72
Soul colour exercise	72
Chakras	73
Thymus chakra	74
Love	76
Universal love exercise	77
Angel healing	79

8 help for others — 81

Watching – Young children	81
Watching – Social	83
Listening – Sensory	84
Listening – Hearing	85
Music – listening exercise	85
Listening – Caring	86
Sharing a centring experience	88
Telepathy	89
Chakra alignment exercise	89
Healing a relationship	91
Universal love exercise	92
What have we learnt?	93
Conclusion	93

further reading — 95

Part 1
about angels

1

introduction to angels

In Malaysia freckles are called angel kisses. How delightful! Anyone who has someone dear to them with freckles must surely be touched by the charm of this saying and the next time you see your freckled someone special you will smile at this memory. The only reason you have not felt this particular delight in freckles before is probably because you did not know the saying. Being touched by angels is a similar experience, they are all around us all the time, we have just not known how to look.

So what *is* an angel? I cannot tell you what an angel is, nor can any other author I have read on the subject. We pose the question and end up telling you what angels do, where they can be found and how others have visualized them. Angelology research, as you will see, has produced all manner of information both factual and hearsay and certainly some books have beautiful illustrations of angels. However, none of us can tell

Angels

you what they actually are, only how others have perceived them.

Interest in angels is usually generated either by people who feel they are in a dark tunnel, or people whose lives have become just a grey tunnel and they begin to wonder 'Is this all there is to it?'. We have all heard about the light at the end of the tunnel and when we see that small light we have something positive to work towards. Many stories which demonstrate angelic intervention involve people who are, or have been, in great pain.

It seems that when one is in total despair, fear or pain, everyday control is suspended. Our minds are busy trying to grapple with the enormity of what is happening. It is often at such times of darkness, when control has slipped, that a space becomes available for divine intervention and a small light appears in the darkness.

With silence only as their benediction God's angels come,
Where, in the shadow of a great affliction, the soul sits dumb.
John Greenleaf Whittier

So where does the darkness go when you switch on the light? It goes nowhere, it was not really there in the first place, although it seemed very real when you were in it. When it is dispelled you realize darkness is an absence not a presence. Knowledge of angels and their support can help you to switch on a light and see into a previously darkened or vacant room of your soul. I have become convinced that angels are an everyday presence and this book sets out to help you find out what an angel is – *for you*.

Positive Loving Thoughts Cast Light

There is great power in both positive and negative thought which can reflect both good and bad upon ourselves and those around us. No matter how hard we try someone will always

introduction to angels

find a negative to your positive. I remember with fondness pointing out to my caustic Granny a beautiful cherry tree covered in blossom. 'Look Gran, isn't that lovely?' 'Yes, but think of the mess it will make when the blossom falls', was her reply. She had had a hard life and that was the way her mind worked. With the light of angels, negative barriers can be gently removed so that you can listen to your true feelings and hear your own intuition guiding you.

Our hectic contemporary lifestyles build barriers just as negative as my Granny's and I suggest we are no more aware of this than she was. If we are ill we go to a doctor and expect to be immediately made better. How many times do you hear people say that they can't take time off work? If we have an emotional crisis we expect to have recovered after six sessions with a counsellor providing the sessions fit in with our work and social calendar, that is.

There is nothing negative in seeking help from doctors or counsellors and accepting their cures. We have come to accept that modern science can deal with certain problems, we take the pills or attend sessions and that's an end to that problem. The negative I am suggesting is that this is only half a cure and usually we just don't think any further. We leave no space for the healing powers of love and time, the protection of instinct.

At least half of any cure is our own responsibility. In order not to keep repeating the same mistakes we need to find our own personal answers to all life's physical, emotional and moral dilemmas. How often do we take time to think through? Why did this calamity happen? How can I prevent it from happening again? Let alone looking at the positive, how can I use this experience to help me in the future? By opening our minds to angels, we can get spiritual guidance to answer these questions, with the added bonus of their comfort and support along the way.

If this book can put across only one idea, I would like it to be that angels and communication with them is as natural and normal as everyday waking and sleeping. For example, to many people swimming is a natural and normal activity but to those who do not like water, and cannot swim, it is not normal. A non-swimmer would rightly ask, why jump into an alien environment and risk drowning? But once you overcome your doubts and learn to swim it becomes an ordinary enjoyable experience. So it is to be in touch with angels.

New experiences are invariably rewarding and, because we are blessed with memory, we carry the results of our experiences with us. From every experience we gain self-knowledge. I used swimming as an analogy because I like water but I am not encouraging non-swimmers to go and jump into the river just for the experience! I am simply proposing that you take a leap of faith which needs just as much courage. We all have a dark side, angels included, as you will see. Self-awareness, warts and all takes courage.

What we hope to achieve through new knowledge and experience is greater pleasure and quality in life for ourselves and others. Once our minds are open to the presence of something special, it can enhance and develop every aspect of our lives.

> *Sometimes it is easier to stay with the devil you know rather than the angel you don't.*
>
> Traditional saying

The Background

With the dawning of a new age of enlightenment our minds are at last opening to accept psychic phenomena not readily explained or proved by science and technology and I am suggesting that we live our daily lives among angels. This book sets out to demonstrate how angels have always been with us. The very fact that you, the reader have chosen this subject, indicates that the light has begun to dawn. Perhaps an in-

introduction to angels

explicable phenomena has occurred? Maybe a little voice has been whispering? Possibly intuition has been working overtime?

As soon as you trust yourself you will know how to live.
J.W. von Goethe

This book does not set out to preach a dogma, 'God' is defined as a notion of universal faith, whatever form of religion or belief. Here a set of proposals is presented in order to ask a series of questions designed to set the reader on a search and to open the mind to the subject.

With the constant advances in education and science we have, maybe, become too sophisticated to have faith in the natural scheme of nature. The proposition I am putting forward is that we exist amongst angels. In order to do this we need to look at different interpretations and before we look at what an angel is, we must look at what it is not.

Ghosts and angels are often confused. In all my research and experience I have never found an instance where an angel or angelic experience has been mistaken for a ghost or ghostly experience. Ghosts are said to be spirits of the dead who have not found rest. In every culture it is agreed that ghosts take their own form, which is always reported as chill, floating and transparent. Ghosts retain their earthly personalities, which can be experienced in form or through mediums with messages both welcome and unwelcome. Angel experiences are distinguished by their light, warmth and above all calm. My conclusion is that ghosts represent cold and angels represent warm. Emotionally or physically I think any reader of this book can distinguish between warmth and chill.

The Book

It is down a long, winding and emotional path that I have travelled to come to terms with my belief that we exist in the presence of angels and I would like to take you along that path

Angels

with me. I made my discoveries in much the same order as this book is set out for you. First came the *What*? as I listened to an increasing number of stories, then came the *Where*? as I began to research angelology and, finally came *How* can I benefit from this knowledge? which leads to what I call angel therapy.

In Part One we will look at how angels use all our senses, conscious and unconscious, to communicate. This is done by recounting stories of people who have had experiences of angels and we will look at a diversity of accounts of angelic occurrences over the centuries to the present day.

Thomas Aquinas, eleventh-century philosopher, liked to be known as the Angelic Doctor and his discourses on angels formed the basis of angel knowledge for several hundred years. He was of the opinion that angels were 'all intellect' and were without matter. Religious art often depicts them as beautiful, winged, gentle faced human creatures. In stark contrast to this the Shaman Indians of Eastern Peru believed some angels came in the form of black winged birds who could be 'foul mouthed and lecherous'! And so we will cherry pick through the centuries to get a glimpse of the breadth and depth of our subject matter.

In order to explain the traditional background and hierarchy of angels we often refer to 'God'. Most Westerners think of angels in terms of Christianity and Judaism. The beauty and universal appeal of angelic association is that it crosses all the boundaries of caste creed and religion. Therefore, when we refer to God, the reader is requested to use 'God' as a euphemism for Faith, Life Energy. P.L. Wilson in his book of angels put it well '. . . Every manifestation of God, every epiphany, must take the form suited to the heart which beholds it'.

The History

This brings us to the angelology part of the book. Fifteenth-century Qabalist scholars constructed a Tree of the Angelic

introduction to angels

World. This is used to introduce the better known angels; Gabriel, Michael, Raphael and Uriel and their perceived functions. Lucifer started out as an angel, it appears he had an attitude problem and we all know where he ended up. The concept of hell is put into context, we all have a dark side.

Sandalphon is the guardian spirit and chief of all guardian angels. There is a system of protection and guidance within us and about us. The Catholic view is that everyone has a guardian no one, good or bad, is left out. It is through the system of guardian angels that we can begin to live with angels.

The Practical

The final part could be specified as angel therapy or simply self-help. The reader is taken slowly and gently along the way to angel contact. Exercises are clear and practical, they require no special skill or previous knowledge, just patience and an open mind. Emphasis is placed on naturalness and enjoyment.

The introductory exercise involves angel cards, their construction and use. The general idea is to use a recognized method of learning and practical involvement with angelic communication. These cards display suggested mantra words, the exercise is in relaxation and concentration. Direction is then focused upon positive meditation and connection with the light, comfort and joy of angelic presence.

The simple gentle exercise practised with angel cards will form the basis of all the other help exercises. In the last section we introduce influences of light and colour. In conjunction with light and colour we look to use chakra energy centres to direct energy to specific areas of our body and our lives. The Thymus chakra is powerful as physically it is said to control the immune system and emotionally it is accepted as the gateway to a universal brotherhood of love and peace. Each exercise will build upon the previous one to give you confidence and experience in angel communication and their healing powers.

2

what is an angel?

The word angel is from the Greek meaning messenger, it is also a generic term for a group or collection of beings. In this chapter we will look into the messenger aspect, how, to whom and through what medium. Each section will look to illustrate, in modern times and terms, how messengers have appeared and what form the message can take.

In quoting angelic experiences we will look to demonstrate how all the senses are used in communication. Here it is suggested that the mythical sixth sense can be recognized and used in appreciating how angles endeavour to communicate with us. The tales are deliberately taken from a wide range and type of people.

A Soldier's Angel – Voices

Brummie Stokes is best known as a mountaineer, a brave and courageous one at that. In his autobiography, *Soldiers and*

What is an Angel?

Sherpas, Brummie recounts his experiences in the British Special Air Service (SAS). His background is of a loving but hard childhood in the north of England. To achieve his ambition to get into the SAS, and subsequently their mountain corps, showed considerable determination and not a little improvisation. Brummie lost half a foot to frostbite, recovered, trained with one boot half filled with sand and then carried on climbing mountains and instructing for the SAS. So here we have a rough, tough professional soldier. Not a man given to fantasy. The incident which interests us took place during jungle warfare in Borneo, where British soldiers were assisting the local government during terrorist troubles.

Brummie is creeping around the jungle doing what soldiers do and, in the process, using his expertise to keep himself and his men alive. The team is on full alert making its way through occupied territory, Brummie in the lead. They are deep within dank undergrowth, the jungle canopy affording only a gloomy light. The tangle of sinewy roots and rotting vegetation making it difficult for the soldiers to move smoothly, each footstep by instinct and training rather than sight.

Brummie, at this stage in his SAS career, is highly experienced and as this mission is fairly routine has no reason not to trust his finely honed skills. Nevertheless, as he carefully advances, he cannot shift a feeling of especial caution. Their pathway is obstructed by a fallen tree trunk and Brummie lifts a leg to step over. As his leg rises a voice in his head says 'don't put your foot down', his neck prickles, his weight shifts and the voice repeats 'don't put your foot down'. Experience has taught Brummie to trust himself and he pulls back from the tree trunk. After some persuasion his bomb disposal men investigate, finding a landmine behind the trunk which would almost certainly have killed Brummie and most of his team.

Later in his career Brummie is caught in a bad storm on Everest, he and his exhausted mate have to spend a second night marooned in inadequate shelter without essential supplies

Angels

and it is essential, if they are to survive, that they stay awake. Brummie reports feeling a presence which accompanied and encouraged him through the long, bitterly cold, night. The men survived the night and eventually made it down the mountain. I am convinced the voice and the subsequent presence during that night were Brummie's guardian angel. He interpreted it as instinct or a sixth sense, which we will discuss later.

> *For the good angel will go with him, his journey will be successful, and he will come home safe and sound.*
>
> Tob 5:21

Fragrance

Shirley is a middle-class, middle-aged housewife, an intelligent independent woman who has run a home and brought up her daughters largely alone whilst her husband worked abroad. Shirley's family were a sporty lot, so she was used to dealing with the inevitable injuries and aching muscles and often used a pungent commercially available heat rub. Her husband finally returned home to stay because he learned that he had cancer. Spending long hours in bed, unable to move much, the poor man's body became stiff and worn. Shirley reverted to her old remedy and massaged his wasted muscles with the heat rub. So she nursed and cared for him until he died of his illness.

Recovering from the tragic death of her husband Shirley resolved to get on with her life. At the time we meet her Shirley's daughters have left home and she is embarking happily upon another relationship. Whilst the girls were at home Shirley had become a consummate family taxi driver so she had no fears about driving. On the night in question she had a long journey to make, it was November and the weather was awful, cold, with sleeting rain. The fact that the narrow winding road was flanked by large trees, their fallen autumn leaves making the road surface treacherous, was not helping her progress. As every

What is an Angel?

driver knows, it was here that she got stuck behind a slow-moving lorry!

Shirley is a good driver, she knew the road and she decided to overtake. Having checked that the road ahead was clear, just as she made the last manoeuvre the car was filled with the unmistakable smell of the heat rub. The aroma was so overwhelming that Shirley fell back behind the lorry she had been following and, as she did so, another large truck hurtled past in the opposite direction. The smell went as quickly as it had appeared but had she overtaken she would surely have been killed. Although Shirley views her story as just one of those things she cannot explain in life, I am quite sure a protector had been sent to her by Raphael. More of him in Part Two.

Angels are often associated with rescue and protection and numerous stories of a similar nature are recorded – see Further Reading at the back of this book. However, the message can be of a different nature, comforting and sometimes poignant as in the following stories.

Dreams

Kath is the matriarch; a large family of children and grandchildren, all of whom are mindful of her sharp tongue and razor wit. This story begins in the 1920s when Kath's inquisitive mind embarked upon the inevitable awkward questions about where did she come from. She was not a child to be fobbed off with the traditional evasive replies. Kath can remember being told that a mother always gets to choose her own baby. Fair enough, but where from? This young woman, true to her later form, is not letting anyone off the hook. 'Well darling, when a man and a woman decide they want a baby an angel comes and takes the woman to a heaven full of children where she can make her choice.' Remember this is the 1920s and sex was not openly talked about, so Kath accepts this as far as it goes; but how?

So Mamma took young Kath upon her knee and told the

Angels

story of her dream. One night an angel visited her and took her to a meadow full of happy children all running free and playing in groups. She watched them all and walked among them talking to some but never seeing the one she wanted. At the end of a meadow was an orchard full of fruit trees in blossom and there, sitting in the fork of a tree, was a sad looking little boy swinging his legs all by himself.

She called to him, asked his name and why he looked unhappy. He smiled sweetly and said he was sad because nobody chose him. Mother said she had already chosen him, what was his name and would he come down to Earth to be with her? He said his name was Peter and he would love to come but he could not stay long, he could only visit. Mother said even if it was only for a short time she would really like him to come. Kath wept – and she never forgot her mother's dream.

Kath tells me that the story was never referred to again and it was many years before she learned that her mother had had a son born before her and that he had lived barely three weeks, just long enough to be christened Peter. At the end of this poignant little tale Kath concluded – I have always understood that Peter Pan would never grow up.

Angel of Mine – A Beautiful Creature

Have you experienced sorrow? Do you recognize that hopeless feeling of abandonment, when a body seems to be sliding into blackness with nothing and nobody to hold on to?

So there was I, sobbing, shaking, shivering, my world shattered. The bitter taste of one's own tears, arms wrapped around oneself so tight it's difficult to breath, despair. Head spinning, neck aching, back breaking, limbs hurting where my own fingers bruise my arms. The dark side urging alcohol, nicotine, head-under-the-covers. The light side whispers from far away, 'the sun is shining.' Dark side 'what good'll that do?' Light side, calmly 'just open the door Lynn.' So we stagger, clutching and choking into the open air.

Now drama dictates I render unto you a tale of golden light, glorious presence and me awakening joyful to spring forth into gladness. Well sorry, we are dealing with real life here in the twenty-first century. What really happened is that I just stood there hunched up, in my mind was a rather childish 'So?' Panic is welling up in the pit of my stomach. What am I going to do? How am I going to cope?

Cool breeze on a hot red cheek tempts me to turn my head. On the fence was a butterfly, a large butterfly. Now I'm no 'Butterflyologist', but I can tell you it was a fairly common sort, just very beautiful. Velvet wings shimmered with jewel colours, edges of delicate lace, decorated with smooth continuous curves of deepest royal purple. In order to watch as my beautiful butterfly shimmied in the sunshine, I had to lift my head. Lifting ones head drops the shoulders, which eases the neck ache and releases the back muscles. I became aware of warmth on the back of my neck which spread down my back. Clenched hands relaxed, clutching replaced by stroking. So we sat together – a beautiful creature and a sad creature.

Gradually the outside world encroached, smells of blossom and next-door's barbecue, sounds of birds and distant aeroplanes. The sun has warmed my body and the seat has numbed my behind (angels can communicate through *all* the senses). Those brilliant wings made a final flutter and lifted gently into the blue sky. Following it up, my gaze found my neighbour at an upstairs window. 'Hi, coming round for a beer and a hello?'

So I turned into the light instead of sliding into the dark. Of course, there were no overnight revelations or dramatic change to my circumstances. What I remember clearly is warmth, physical warmth, but also emotional warmth. I was no longer alone with my burden. I still don't know anything about butterflies, but I've never seen another so beautiful.

Angels

However, every time I see a butterfly I smile, say hello and carry with me that lovely feeling of comfort and compassion.

The final story in this section also involves angel intervention in time of danger, somewhat different in that it involves more than one person. Several people witnessed this incident which was widely reported at the time and is recorded in G.S. Eckersley's comprehensive book of angelic experiences, *Angel at my Shoulder*.

Protection

Lee Abbey is an Anglican retreat centre set beside the cliffs in rolling Devon countryside, with extensive tourist facilities and chalets available for visitors to rent. In the middle of summer visitors are plentiful and the farmers busy about their fields so that by lunchtime all were converging on the same area across the car park looking for food and a rest from their labours. Children, happy and excited, urging their parents to the inevitable ice-cream van, farm labourers from the fields looking forward to a cool glass of cider and inhabitants of the chalets on the cliff side, setting up their barbecues.

A bright yellow tractor was parked at the top of a slope leading to the crowded car park. Its driver climbed out thankfully and joined the throng drifting towards the cafeteria complex. Glancing back the driver was horrified to see his tractor rolling with increasing speed towards the crowds. As the vehicle gathered momentum there was little he could do except shout warnings to the families, who could only stand immobilized with fear as they watched the yellow monster thundering towards them. Suddenly, and for no apparent reason, the huge wheels veered abruptly right, the tractor narrowly missing the crowd, as it now hurtled towards one of the holiday chalets.

Andrew, who had watched in horror from a chalet, was now in its immediate path. What to do? Where to run? He was

What is an Angel?

helpless in the face of such peril. As Andrew's mind whirled, the tractor once again, for no reason and going far too fast for anything to deflect it, turned sharply and missed Andrew and his family by a few metres before tipping onto its side and demolishing the family car.

Monks and other courageous men rushed down the cliff intent, as they thought, on rescuing Andrew's family and the tractor driver. However, their brave attempts were in vain, for when the cab was opened there was not a person to be seen, nor had anyone been thrown clear. Andrew, who remember had been in the vehicle's path for those few awful seconds, and monks who had also witnessed the headlong plunge were quite sure they had seen a silhouette in the cab. Yet the driver had left the cab and, in any case, the speed and momentum of the tractor would have made steering far too heavy for human strength. This all happened well over a decade ago and still no one has come up with an earthly explanation.

> *Believe me that an Angel's hand is there*
> Fra Giovanni

So what is an angel? Great philosophers over the centuries have argued that question, so I would not presume to make a judgment, but as we have seen here they are indeed comforters and protectors, especially in times of need.

3
image of angels

That's all an Angel is; an idea of God –

Eckhart

Having looked briefly at what angels are, the conclusion reached was actually more related to what they do. Here we take up the concept of angel messengers and look at suggested form and appearance. We have beautiful recorded descriptions of Seraphim with three pairs of scarlet wings and swords of flaming red and Kerubim richly garbed in royal blue. Michael is represented in human form, strong young and handsome, a radiant warrior. In the Bible angels are seen to possess a spiritual nature and yet they assume such human characteristics as voices; heavenly choirs being a common concept.

Philosophers

Through the ages there are well-recorded debates by theologians, philosophers and mystics questioning how a being can take a shape but, from all accounts, lack a material nature. Maimonides, a medieval Jewish philosopher, surmised that all angelic appearances were 'figurative expressions' or, in modern terms, wish fulfilment. Thomas Aquinas took this concept a step further and referred to angels as powers of immaterial spirits. He also refers to 'a succession of contacts of power at diverse places'. All of which tie in with the experiences recorded in Chapter 2.

Emanuel Swedenborg, eighteenth-century Swedish theologian and scientist, spent the last 25 years of his life studying and writing many books on his own experiences and theories of angels. His doctrines have influenced some of the great poets including Blake and von Goethe. The scientist Swedenborg also wrote that angels were not of a material nature because they did not reflect the sun's rays. He therefore concluded that we see angels through the soul, or inward eye, in direct proportion to the ability of the individual to receive goodness and truth. Or maybe a sixth sense?

Religion

It is from the history and art of Christianity and Judaism that we get our richest source of visual representations, always showing angels busily commuting between God and man. Old testament angels, as they appeared in a dream to Isaac's son Jacob, were described in human form with no wings or colourful garb, climbing a ladder between heaven and earth. Jacob's Ladder took its place in angelology as the recognized route travelled by heavenly messengers on their errands of goodwill. In his Old Testament vision the prophet Ezekiel saw angels in the form of a winged wheel with bright eyes around the circumference.

Angels

Confusingly these wheels are also referred to as thrones or mounts for the Kerubim and Seraphim. I would interpret this as meaning that the wheels/thrones are both the message and the messenger, rather like our computers today. This idea came from seeing an illustration of Adolphe N. Dudron's in his 'Christian Iconography' showing the wings as little hooks grappling along Jacob's Ladder, rather like a child's toy. According to the Bible the wheels traverse a heavenly expanse of 'terrible crystal' and settle in sapphire rings around the throne of Metatron.

Through the ages descriptions of angels grew more extravagant and more indistinct, frequently having multiple roles and appearances, which could well have led to the philosophy of angels being an idea or a dream. To illustrate such duplication let us look at descriptions of Metatron, the highest of all angels. At the same time he has been described as an ancient bearded humanoid prophet and a radiantly beautiful celestial youth suffused by rainbows. We can look at this in two ways, that he started as a radiant youth and matured extravagantly, or travelled a mystic route from the plain reproduction humans of Jacob's first vision and ascended to the magnificent celestial model described by the fifteenth-century Qabalist monks.

The good and the true of all denominations have recorded their own definitions through the centuries. Mohammed, a great prophet who received the words of the Koran from Gabriel believed that nothing could occur without the presence of angels, that we exist because of this phenomena, he preached that every drop of rain was accompanied by an angel, therefore the crops grew and the rivers ran.

This belief could be said to arise from the legend of how Gabriel came to Mohammed. He came upon 1,600 wings that stretched from east to west. Legend gives him saffron hair, yellow feet and green wings, his neck hung with rubies and a face of radiant brightness. Each day he entered the ocean 360 times and when he came out each wing shed a million drops of water and each drop became an angel.

Water as an element of creation, based securely in anthropology, appears constantly in mystic legend, a favourite of mine is that of Islamic paradise. It is said to be inhabited by the good and faithful who have taken the form of emerald birds living in golden pavilions. These pavilions line the green shaded banks of crystal waters, which flow in abundance into streams and, when a golden goblet is dipped into the stream, the water becomes wine. This wine which we are told never begets weightiness is imbibed by the inhabitants whilst reclining at leisure in the embrace of a beloved spouse. This imagery is much frowned upon by Christians and Muslims particularly, theologians are at pain to point out that these pleasures are only to be enjoyed in the next life as a reward to those who have abstained in this life!

This traditional Islamic fable dispels the popular misconception that Islam prohibits images. I have found Islamic sources rich in celestial imagery. Israfil, for instance, has dual functions of Angel of Day and Angel of Music. He is described as having abundant hairs and numerous tongues beneath outspread veils. With each tongue he can speak a thousand languages. As he sings the praises of Allah from each breath an angel is created. Every day and very night Israfil approached the gates of hell with his songs to try to convert the wicked in the name of Allah, however his song remained unheard and he became pale and thin, until he was but the radius of a bowstring. Although not too successful in this instance again we see the messenger and multiplication or, more simply, creation theme again.

Five thousand years after Israfil Allah created Mika'il, he also has green wings and hair of saffron from his head to his toes. Each hair is described as having a million faces. From all the million tongues comes another million languages and every eye wept 70,000 tears. Each tear becomes the Kerubim who bow over the earth and nourish the fruit and the flowers and crops and the trees with, what I assume to be, water and light, the two essential ingredients for any growth.

Primitive

Angelic lore is such a glorious mixture it is impossible to set the boundaries between theology, philosophy, history and good old-fashioned folk lore. In this section we look at the Shaman Indians of Eastern Peru and the Tlingit of Northwest America. Living closer to the earth their mode of transporting spirits from the heavens to earth is more practical; wings, smoke and a pole. Although they appear somewhat tougher the Indian spirits retain angelic characteristics of colourful messengers moving between heaven and earth, carrying blessings.

Although there are records of angels taking human form the Shaman lore relies heavily on birds who are often depicted with rather fierce human faces. Koakiti is a hawk said to appear only to a pure Shaman as a winged man. He comes to the aid of the needy on a magic bridge of tobacco smoke, this bridge is also used to transport the souls of the dead to heaven. Given the local flora and fauna one wonders just what tobacco they were smoking! I think this theory ties up neatly with the philosophy of angels being ideas or dreams. More innocently, the Hummingbirds who have no name, descend in groups, they are said to be without blemish and hover over all the brothers. They come to sing long repetitive choruses which soothe and comfort during the rains.

Duplication of form and appearance is seen once again in Raven, the original and greatest Shaman, whose first manifestation is that of a bird. However, in order to pursue the secrets of humankind he requires many disguises. Along his journeying he is once and again a beautiful boy; a wrinkled old woman with a long sharp nose (bird like?) and a frighteningly ugly old man whose dense beard is likened to fungus. His travels take

Image of Angels

Raven over many heavens and many worlds which he records by carving symbols on tree trunks. The knowledge gathered will, Raven believes, one day give his people the secret of eternal life. This information must be protected and passed only to genuine shamans, therefore the true meaning of his symbols is clear only to true shamans (like Koakiti the hawk).

As time passes and his spiritual travels become ever more convoluted, Raven must ensure his people do not get lost when following his instructions so he made the carved tree trunks into a long pole – a Totem Pole, which for ever more will provide a bridge for shamans upon their cosmic journey. I think we see here the parallel to Jacob's Ladder, the tradition of angelic guidance and protection and, as in Islamic paradise, the eventual reward for those good and faithful to their beliefs.

Modern

We cannot leave angel images without taking a brief look at the United Kingdom's most famous angel; Antony Gormley's sculpture *Angel of the North*. Whilst its conception and construction are soundly based in modern science and technology, I think we can still see represented the traditions of angel lore. This is one of the largest sculptures in Britain and, as far as we know, the biggest angel sculpture in the world. It is situated on an old pit site in Gateshead marking the southern entry to Tyneside. *Angel of the North* is made from 200 tonnes of steel built 54 metres high in the form of a human figure with wings comparable in size to those of a jumbo jet.

This is a public work, commissioned, funded and supported by local and national organizations from school children to national art foundations. The project alone shows a caring nature, involving as it did thousands of people from all walks of life, industrial funding and environmental reclamation. An aura of protection comes from this massive silhouette surveying the landscape, its wings tilted forward in what Antony describes as an embrace. To complete the traditional analogy he even has the rich garb: 'The Angel will also have a warm, appealing colour . . . The surface oxidises to form a patina which mellows with age to a rich red.'

Angels may deliver messages from the realms of glory – or they may work unsung, unseen in ways we can only begin to think about.

Tim Jones

Part 2
angelology

As you become more familiar with this subject, as I hope you will after reading this guide, you will see that angelology is by no means an exact science. May I, therefore, preface Part Two with an appeal to my readers to be tolerant of the apparent vagaries and contradictions which inevitably occur in this ancient subject.

Nine orders of angels.
Sketch from miniature from The Breviary of St Hildegarde, twelfth century

4

tree of the angelic world

Gabriel told Mohammed that God is veiled by 70,000 veils, of light and darkness, and if these were swept aside even He would be consumed. God does not communicate directly with mortals, He does it through a recognized hierarchy. Evidence of its exact structure is confusing to say the least.

Malcolm Godwin put it nicely;

> *Italian bureaucracy is claimed to be the closest to that of Heaven; it works soley by Divine Intervention and takes Eternity for anything to happen. One glimpse into the celestial archives certainly makes anyone wonder just what might occur in an emergency.*
>
> An Endangered Species

For the sake of clarity we will stick to the general order subscribed to by Thomas Aquinas, and later beautifully illustrated by the Qabalist Monks in their Tree of the Angelic World

Tree of the Angelic World

showing nine choirs. The choirs (or orders) are split into groups of three; each group of three forms what is referred to as a Triad:

First Triad

1 **Seraphim** – keepers of divine love. They have six glowing red wings; when they appear in human form two wings cover the face, two the feet and two are used for flying. They carry swords of flaming red, the Fires of Love. The Seraphs are in direct communication with God and chant continuous praises of Holy, Holy, Holy, which vibrates at very high frequencies. This is said to be the vibration of Love, the creation of Life (remember the Hummingbirds?).

2 **Kerubim** (Cherubim) – keepers of wisdom. They are richly dressed in deepest blue, the cloth of bishops. The swords of the Kerubim are ever turning to enable them to guard the way to the Tree of Life at the East Gate of Eden, where they were placed by God. In the original Hebrew form Kerubim were mighty guardians protecting the celestial corridors. They are also depicted as Charioteers of God, the vibrations of their wheels echoing the Seraphim but at a lower rate.

3 **Ophanim** – This is the formal name in the context of Triads for the Thrones or Wheels we met earlier. If the Kerubim are the Charioteers, the Ophanim are the Chariots. This agrees with Jacob's vision of the Wheels and of them being message and messenger. We have to accept that Ophanim, Chariots and vibrations are one and the same and, from these vibrations, can now begin interpretation of the message passing down through the choirs. It can be said that in the third choir is the beginning of the ladder from Heaven to Earth.

Angels

Wheels – Thrones – Ophanim – Third choir

There is a complicated hypothesis of the first three choirs, from whence I suggest our earlier philosophers could have constructed their theories of angels being intellect. It runs along the lines of the thought slowing to become light, then heat, then something to do with condensation into matter. I prefer to think in much simpler terms. Picture the whole cosmos as a pond. Into the centre of the pond is dropped a stone (i.e. the Source of Love, Light and therefore Life), the ripples forming ever increasing circles until they reach the shore. We on the shore may not know where the stone came from, maybe that is what the first Triad tells us, that the secret of eternal life is not available to mortals – yet.

Second Triad

The least known of the angelic Hierarchy, their chief function is to form a pivot or balance between those nearest to God, the first Triad and those nearest to man, the third Triad.

Tree of the Angelic World

Descriptions of the second Triad come mostly as a group, their uniform consisting of long albs, golden girdles and green stoles.

4 **Dominions** – (Lords) Regulators; Channels of Mercy. This is said to be the sphere which holds the holy directions or letters. Dominions could be likened to Justice. I say this because they are illustrated as holding a staff in one hand balanced by a seal in the other, a similar concept to the scales of justice. Christians singing hymns praising the 'Lord of Lords' refer to the Dominions.

5 **Virtues** – for once a name that is self-explanatory! The Virtues bestow heavenly grace and blessings via the angels of the third Triad. Virtues are associated with the struggle for good over evil, they grant to their 'Brilliant and Shining Ones' the courage and compassion to perform great deeds. It is from the Virtues that come the miracles granted to humankind.

6 **Powers** – Balance. Conscience. The Powers can be said to be the keepers of our souls. If the Kerubim guard the Tree of Life, the Powers guard the park borders. Their task is to prevent evil from entering the Kingdom of Heaven. It is in sixth choir that lies the greatest risk of corruption and therefore it is from here we get the 'fallen angels'.

Balance and reconciliation is the prime consideration within this group. The second Triad is obviously related to morality and what it says is that we have a choice.

Third Triad

The practical order, this Triad could be seen as the celestial workforce or more appropriately army, because they are dressed in soldier's uniform decorated with golden sashes and carrying

Angels

weapons such as javelins and axes. Carrying guidance from the first and second Triads, the third Triad dispenses heavenly blessing on earth.

7 **Principalities** – (Princedoms). Another order bearing the name of its function. The Principalities can be said to be the Governors or organizers. They give strength and guidance to their nominees. The Principalities divided the heavens into quarters and nominated rulers.

8 **Archangels** – It is in the eighth order we come to distinguish individuals. Each of the above is recognized as an Archangel, they carry the Divine Decrees from the Principalities. The eighth order is also known as The Magnificent Seven. At least three respectable sources disagree on the number and the names of the Archangels of the eighth choir. In the Book of Revelation the seven angels who stood before God are accepted as Archangels. Christian and Jewish faiths accept that there are seven Archangels; however, they cannot agree on who the seven are (this is one of the reasons why seven is a mystic or lucky number). Muslims take their definitive source as the Koran, in which four Archangels are mentioned, but only two are named; Michael and Gabriel.

9 **Angels** – Here in the ninth choir we arrive at the actual workforce or foot soldier, those closest to us, who are trusted with the divine blessing sent from the universe to humans. It is from the ninth choir that we eventually arrive at the modern concept of angels. Most popular of all are the guardian angels who come to us from these ranks. The ninth choir constitutes the intermediary between God and humankind on earth and from historical records has done so down through the ages.

Tree of the Angelic World

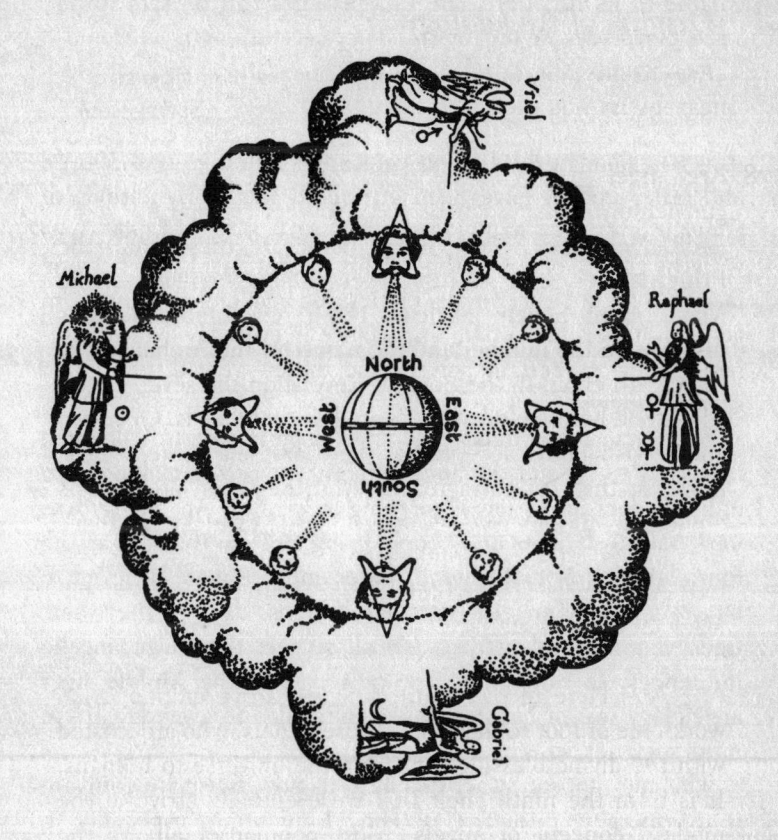

Rulers of spiritual space sketch from: Four Archangels of the Twelve Winds. 1629 Robert Fludd – *Medicina Catholica*

Angels

At the height of its popularity in what in known as the 'high' Middle Ages, our Qabalist monks were quoting 301,655,722 angels, all of whom were said to be named and chronicled, although I cannot in all honesty say I have seen this evidence!

Origins of Angelology

Every visible thing in this world is put in charge of an angel.
St Augustine

Angels appear in the Roman catacombs dated around 300 CE and other images have been attributed to the Byzantines of Constantine the Great. However, it was in the Middle Ages with the growth of the Catholic Church that angelology became fashionable; not only among clerics and academics, but also in general. Angels took on an importance in everyday lives of ordinary people as certain powers and duties were attributed to specific angels.

Such was the influence of angelology that it was deemed necessary to consult the angelic 'Thinkers' before making even ordinary decisions such as planting or herding. Angelology was important to farmers and people living close to the land as the four elements of earth, wind, water and fire were believed to be governed by angels. Astrological signs, days of the week, trees, animals and plants were all subject their own angelic influences, so throughout the best part of the Middle Ages angelology was of considerable significance to everyday life in most societies.

This may appear rather quaint to us now, but if we compare it to emerging influence of Feng Shui today, especially in Eastern industrial powers we can see a remarkable comparison. In Hong Kong, Tokyo or Seoul powerful business conglomerates will not build offices or factories, let alone airports and towns without consulting a Feng Shui expert. Pascal said 'If there is a God, better off paying ones dues if not, there's nothing

Tree of the Angelic World

to lose'. Now whether these two widely spaced societies were just hedging their bets I wouldn't like to say, but it takes a brave man to ignore the popular philosophies of their day.

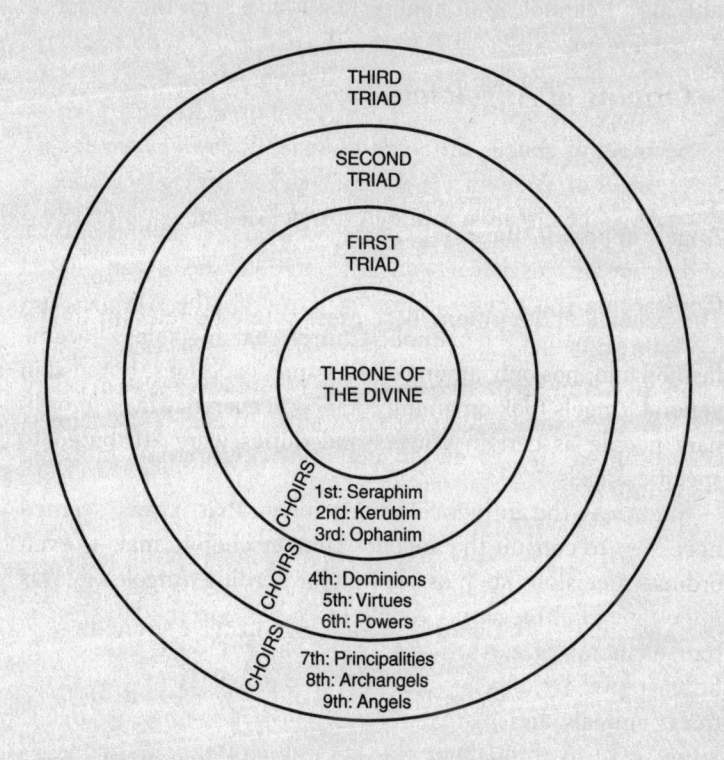

```
            THIRD
            TRIAD

            SECOND
            TRIAD

            FIRST
            TRIAD

          THRONE OF
          THE DIVINE

       CHOIRS  1st: Seraphim
               2nd: Kerubim
               3rd: Ophanim

       CHOIRS  4th: Dominions
               5th: Virtues
               6th: Powers

       CHOIRS  7th: Principalities
               8th: Archangels
               9th: Angels
```

Hierarchy of angels

Of course, in the Middle Ages we are not talking about building towns and factories, but it is interesting to look at what aspects were considered important and how it relates to the present day.

You may be familiar with the ancient Chinese belief of equal and opposite Yin and Yang (for instance male and female). Celestial influence or forces are said to create magnetic fields that flow around us – (this will become more relevant later

Angels

when we look at Chakras), these magnetic fields or cosmic forces are grouped into equal and opposite pairs:

Heaven	Earth
Heavenly Father	Earthly Mother
Angel of Love	Angel of Water
Angel of Peace	Angel of Joy
Angel of Wisdom	Angel of Air
Angel of Creative Work	Angel of Life

The balance and harmony here must surely be relevant to any age or society.

Of the seven Archangels mentioned there was a system called the Essene System which assigned a day to each angel (this is according to the seven angels in the Christian morning communion):

Day	Angel	Gift
Monday	Gabriel	Angel of Life, give strength to my whole body
Tuesday	Camael	Angel of Joy, give beauty to all living things
Wednesday	Raphael	Angel of Sun, give the fire of Life; to the whole body
Thursday	Sachiel	Angel of Water, give the water of life to the whole body
Friday	Anael	Angel of Air, give the air of life to the whole body
Saturday	Cassiel	She gives the food of life to the whole body

Tree of the Angelic World

Sunday	Michael	Angel of Earth, enter the generative organs and regenerate the whole body

Major celestial bodies had their own governors:

This shows another grouping of 'The Magnificent Seven' containing only three of our seven.

Angel	Planet	Angel	Planet
Raphael	Sun	Gabriel	Moon
Sammael	Mars	Michael	Mercury
Zidkiel	Venus	Hanael	Saturn
Kepharel	Jupiter		

Astrologers also assigned angelic governors:

Angel	Sign	Month
Gabriel	Aquarius	January
Barchiel	Pisces	February
Machidiel	Aries	March
Asmodel	Taurus	April
Ambriel	Gemini	May
Muriel	Cancer	June
Verchiel	Leo	July
Hamaliel	Virgo	August
Uriel	Libra	September
Barbiel	Scorpio	October
Adnachiel	Sagittarius	November
Hanael	Capricorn	December

Angels

In Chapter 3 we looked at duplication of form and appearance, to conclude this section we look at duplication of duties in the equal and opposite sense. Here we have The Magnificent Seven again though in some cases by a different name. Where the trees fit in will be familiar to those readers conversant with the Language of Trees. This is just another small instance which supports our opening theory that knowledge of angels can enhance ones pleasure in something previously accepted as fairly ordinary.

Angel	Yin Yang Charge	Tree
Gabriel	Warm or Scorch	Broom
Michael	Make wise or foolish	Almond
Sammael	Strengthen or weaken	Oak
Zadkiel (Kepharel)	Make whole or accursed	Pomegranate
Kafziel (Hanael)	Grant or withhold the heart's desire	Quince
Aniel (Zidkiel)	Make fruitful or barren	Terebinth

Special Functions

As with the Saints, there are specific angels said to be responsible for specific duties.

Chemistry (or Alchemy as it was known) – Och
Water (Aquarius) – Ausiel
Maths (Calculations) – Butator
Dawn – Luchifer (alias Samuel)

Tree of the Angelic World

Fear – Yroul
Forgetfulness – Poteh
Hail – Barbiel
Insomnia – Michael
Mountains – Rampel
Patience – Achaiah
Pride – Rahab
Showers – Zaafdiel
Strength – Zeruel
Bareness – Akiel
Chance – Barakeil
Dreams – Gabriel
Food – Manna
Freewill – Tabris
Health – Mumiah
Lust – Priapus
Music – Israfel
Plants – Sachluph

Rain – Matriel
Silence – Shateiel
Thunder – Ramiel
Birds – Arael
Conception – Laila
Earthquakes – Rashiel
Forests – Zulphas
Future – Teiaiel
Hope – Phanuel
Morals – Mehabish
Night – Leliel
Poetry – Uriel
Rivers – Dara
Snow – Shalgiel
Vegetables – Sofiel
and last but not least
an angel of Water
Insects – Shaziel

Before we leave angelology, a brief look at another 'ology'. The etymology of the angel's names reveals a fascinating insight into the knowledge and dedication of the original angelologists. Every Archangel name, you may have noticed ends in *el*, an ancient word indicating singular. Some works refer to the angels by the older spelling (e.g. Micha-el or Uri'el). However, there is only one angel Michael, one Uriel, etc. They may go by other names, but no two angels carry the same name, hence the *el*; a single entity. Also it is interesting to note translation into different languages remained true to the original intention. El/Ellu in Sumerian and Babylonian means brightness or shining one, in Anglo-Saxon it means radiant being, in Welsh, Irish and Old English is also means shining or shining being.

Angels

Think when the sun shines how it sparkles on the sea, mountains, on the snow and in the rain, radiant dawns and sun sets, surely we are surrounded by shining things? A lovely light quote to end this rather heavy chapter:

> *Outside the open window the morning air is all awash with angels.*
> *Love Calls Us to the Things of This World*, Richard Wilbur

5

knowledge of angels

Knowledge of Angels

Having looked at how they are organized and introduced several names, we will now take a few of the better-known angels and get to know more about them. In no special order, we start with Michael because he is 'drop-dead' gorgeous.

Michael – Prince of Light

To recap some of the things we have already learned about Michael, he is one of the four named Archangels and one of only two mentioned in the Old Testament. He is the angel of the Sabbath day, he rules the almond trees of the earth and is responsible for the balance between wisdom and foolishness. Michael is ruler of the planet Mercury, he is also Angel of the

Angels

Earth and can be invoked to regenerate the whole body, which could marry up to his specific responsibility for helping insomniacs. What is more regenerative and natural than sleep?

Michael is God's champion, his name means 'who is of God'. Michael is said to have disposed single handedly of a huge Assyrian army threatening Jerusalem, which is why he is known as the patron of Israel. He is depicted in the male human form as a glorious warrior, with peacock wings, dressed in shining armour carrying an unsheathed sword. At his feet often lies a slain serpent. It was Michael who subdued the dragon Satan and banished him from heaven in single combat. The popular dragon story is the one for which he competes in history with St George.

The version I much prefer is as follows.

The ninth-century legend of St David has Michael using cunning (or wisdom?), rather than weapon, to dispose of the serpent who was wreaking havoc amongst all the heavenly creatures with his enormous appetite for food and evil. The gentle St David, after some complex negotiations, got the dragon to agree to leave the kingdom peaceably promising to escort him personally to safety. The dragon it appears was afraid of thunder!

So off they set for the coast, St David firmly holding the dragon's hand, not taking his eyes off his charge. Michael shouted 'Hey Dave', St David turned around. Bang. The dragon was struck by lightening. One large smouldering heap of dragon. David was, naturally, a bit upset and Michael explained that had the dragon entered the water he would have multiplied to such an extent that all God's kingdoms would have been devastated. Banished dragons are said to be the origin of the Michael's Mounts seen on the coasts of Europe.

Gabriel – Angel of Humanity

When an angel appears to humans he is sent by Gabriel, the second angel mentioned in the Old Testament. As we have seen, Gabriel is ruler of the moon, sun sign Aquarius, he is the angel of life who gives strength to our whole body, his given day is Monday, his tree the Broom and the harmony between warmth and scorch. He came to the prophet Mohammed in all his glory to reveal the words of the Koran and thereby became known also as the Angel of Truth. In the Qabalist icon of the Tree of Life he stands between Michael and Sandalphon and is shown as a beautiful young boy, dressed in green silk, holding a golden horn to his lips. Gabriel will often send messages through dreams.

There is a respected but controversial school of thought which identifies Gabriel as a female angel. The only female to appear in the first eight choirs. Some evidence for this lies in her being placed at the right hand of God. She appears in many instances of conception. She announced the coming of a Messiah to Daniel and the birth of John the Baptist to Zacharias. Further evidence is that when Gabriel appeared to the Virgin Mary she 'was filled with terror and consternation and could not reply, she had never been greeted by a man before'. It was only when Mary realized this was a female that she calmed and accepted the news being imparted.

In Simone Martini's beautiful picture, simply titled *Gabriel* we see a gentle female holding a lily, the symbol of immaculate conception. The moon also indicates the feminine. Gabriel is perhaps best known as the Angel of Annunciation. Gabriel is chief of all guardian angels, a new baby's birth guardian is nominated by Gabriel. However for the sceptics Gabriel is also interpreted as meaning 'Divine Husband'.

Raphael – Divine Physician

This merciful and good humoured angel is said to be set over all the diseases and wounds of adults and children. He is best known as the Angel of Healing. As we have seen, his planet is the sun, hence a further title as regent or angel of the sun, maybe it is from here he gets his reputation for having a sunny disposition. Noah received from Raphael the book of knowledge he needed to build the Ark, giving Raphael further status as the Angel of Science and Knowledge. He was also a proficient apothecary.

In the guise of Azarias 'a man of good reputation' Raphael volunteered to accompany Tobias, son of Tobit on a business trip. Tobit, a good and faithful man was a rich and respected merchant even though he was blind. During their journey Ararias instructed young Tobias in the art of fishing and preservation of the fish heart, liver and gall for their 'magic properties'. When they eventually arrived in Persia Tobias met and fell for one Sara. However, he was a bit concerned (understandably) to learn that she had had seven previous husbands, all of whom came to a nasty end on their wedding night before their union had been consummated.

Azarias persuaded Tobias to have faith and that all would be well if he burned the heart and liver of the fish in his bridal chamber. Sure enough Tobias and Sara spent a blissful night and went on to live happily ever after. In the meantime Azarias attended to his business and everyone returned to Tobit rejoicing. Before taking his leave Azarias instructed Tobias to make a poultice of the fish gall and lay it upon his father's eyes. Tobit thereby regained his sight and offered Azarias half of his considerable wealth in thanks. Azarias refused and revealed himself as Raphael, one of the seven Archangels sent by the holy one to reward his servants on earth.

Uriel – Angel of Repentance

I introduce Uriel here to bring about some balance and, curiously, Uriel rules the sign of Libra which are represented by the scales. Angels are not all sweetness and light, there is a tough and disciplinarian side to them as perhaps there has to be in any hierarchy. His name means 'Fire of God' and Uriel is the president of hell, who guards the Gates of Eden with a fiery sword. This pitiless angel watches over thunder and terror and anyone who is heard to blaspheme is warned they will be hanged by their tongues!

None can expect to escape scrutiny, Uriel is sharp-eyed and quick of wit. He is wise to our tricks, maybe because he was one of the first angels to become human. In the prayer of Joseph Uriel says 'I have come down to earth to make my dwelling among men, and I am called Jacob by name.' There is a report of one Jacob wrestling with the dark angel at the gates of heaven and Uriel is the favourite candidate for this role. Uriel is fair; he did warn Noah of the coming of the floods. He is firm; he chastised Moses for failing to observe the subscribed rites of circumcision. Be warned.

Yet Uriel is also the Angel of Poetry – poetic justice I wonder?

Metatron – Angel of the Lord

The prophet Enoch who became an angel. Although there are many contenders for the title of Greatest Angel, in most accounts Metatron is granted the title of the highest, he sits at the right hand of God and is often referred to as simply The Lord. As mentioned earlier he is described at once as ancient and bearded and as a radiant youth. Metatron is the heavenly scribe. When on earth as the prophet Enoch he was chosen by God as writer of the truth. At God's request Michael stripped him of his clothes, anointed him with oil, scented him with myrrh until he shone like a sunbeam and Enoch was then transformed into a fiery angel with six wings on the left, six on the right and countless eyes.

Other titles ascribed to Metatron are Prince of the Divine Face, Angel of the Covenant and King of Angels. However, this is a mighty and terrible angel, he is said to be closest to God and, in common with Uriel, there are stories of his wreaking terrible vengeance in the name of righteousness. The passage in Exodus about sending an angel to keep thee in the way of the Lord thy God is attributed to Metatron. He is understood in some circles to be the female principle in God. So here we have a balance again. Perhaps the hold 'radiant youth/ancient bearded' can be interpreted as 'an old head on young shoulders'?

Sandalphon – Guardian Spirit

This is a vast gentle soul, whose height is said to extend upward throughout the universe and taller 'by a journey of five hundred years than any other'. The very name sounds like the sound of approaching footsteps. Said in some accounts to be the twin of Metatron, this is the other chief of all guardian angels. We don't hear a lot about Sandalphon, but I find him/her enormously reassuring. My interpretation of twin is that here we have again a balance; the heavy-handed Metatron and the gentle Sandalphon, who could be seen as the feminine principle. Heavenly father, earthly mother?

Samuel – Angel of Evil

Alias Lucifer, Satan and Iblis. Once the favourite of God, Lucifer is variously known as morning star, prince of morning, lord of light. His is both the morning and evening star because he has the ability, like a reptile (serpent), to shed his skin and appear renewed and unrecognizable to the unsuspecting. In the book of Job, Lucifer is described as an elegant, sardonic adversary, strolling around heaven playing games of chances with God. There are two popular accounts of his downfall.

The first is another infamous story of Michael and the dragon. Apparently there was a mighty struggle in heaven between Michael and the serpent Satan, which saw Michael triumphing and Lucifer falling 'like lightening from heaven' to quote the Book of Luke, taking numerous bad angels with him.

It took Lucifer nine days to recover, than he set about Adam and Eve in Paradise, the story of which is told in Milton's *Paradise Lost* and described in Dante's *Inferno*. So Hell was established, with its whole hierarchy of demons.

The second story is much more gentle. After God had created the heavens and all its angels, He carried on to complete the plan by creating humankind and instructed his Angels to nurture and serve them. Samuel (as he still was) protested he loved God best and his sole charge was to serve God and he could serve no other. Samuel persisted in his refusal to bow to humans even on behalf of God, at which God lost his patience and commanded Samuel 'Get out of my sight'.

Lucifer was instantly cast into Hell, the hell of being parted from one's beloved, the only way he could cope was to hold in his heart that he was bidden to such a place by God, whom he would continue to serve by creating a bridge between good and evil. As Jakob Bohome, in Mysterium Magum, puts it: 'Thus we are to understand that Evil and Good Angels dwell near to one another, . . . For heaven is in Hell and Hell is in Heaven.' Or, in modern terms, one man's heaven is another man's hell.

The Feminine Principle

The first angels illustrated were male. From the earliest times, through to fifteenth-century Renaissance certainly, in painting and sculpture we see representation of the naked male body. Christian and Islam angels were not described as masculine or feminine. If seen as intellect, ideas or dreams, angels are then passive. Because they represent completion; perfection and dimensions beyond our imagination, angels are generally taken as androgynous. However, the feminine ideal cannot be ignored, especially as Wisdom is a feminine principle.

Angels

Sophia – Angel of Wisdom

Here we have another contender for greatest angel, Sophia is known as the angel Aeon (of immense time). She is said to have given birth to all the other angels, being both mother and lover. In Christianity, although she is much exalted, it is made clear that she is not above the Virgin Mary. She is depicted like the Seraphim suffused in crimson, seated upon a throne. The crimson aura can be interpreted as representing dawn, or the transposition between two worlds.

Sophia's lover sons became obsessed by the magic of sexual union. Sophia tired of them and endeavoured to find a way to create without male union. This caused great anger among her male counterparts and she was spitefully cast into a world of rape and humiliation. In this role she became keeper of profane and carnal knowledge. With patience she endured and concentrated upon pursuing the light of the absolute.

Her tormentors eventually conceded Sophia's knowledge and endurance and she was restored to heaven to become the greatest of all angels. Her conclusion recorded in the scrolls of the Dead Sea. 'I am the first and the last, the honoured and the despised, the whore and the holy one, wife and virgin, barren and fertile.'

Sounds about right to me.

Israfil – Angel of Judgment Day

Rather than greatest, Israfil aspires to be the mightiest of angels. He sits in a golden glow and presides over a host of prophets. His home is in the heaven of the sun which was created for him from the light of the heart. He is of wondrous size, his head brushing the heavens his feet beneath the earth. Of his four wings, two cover east and west, one is his protection the last covers his body. His popular image is that of presiding over the Resurrection with Gabriel. He blows a mighty trumpet to awaken the spirits so all may be raised to heaven. Together with Gabriel's horn we have the origins of the resurrection music.

With some relief here we are at the end of this rather weighty section. Confused? If so, welcome to a company of great minds and brains. On a positive note, the aggregation of guises and roles reassures us that there can be no right or wrong way to approach or use angelology. To misquote Peter Wilson 'Every manifestation of Angels, every epiphany, must take the form suited to the heart which beholds it.'

The true angel is the one *you* experience.

Part 3
working with angels

*Be not afraid to have
Strangers in your house,
for some thereby have
entertained angels unawares.*
                    Heb. 13:2

6

angel calling cards

A basic exercise used in all celestial communication, splits broadly into two parts: preparation then relaxation, leading to meditation then communication. Small cards are used as a learning tool to focus on the broad concept of angel assistance. Each card carries a word to be used for meditation. The actual making of the cards is used as a gentle introduction to the simplicity and stillness required. A list of 'essence' words is suggested. First, we look at the concept of asking not demanding, then at the role of intuition in the exercise. The final part of the exercise involves focusing and accepting, responding and, finally, allowing the changes to take place.

There are many ways to work with angels, connecting with them puts us in touch with a universal mind of greatness and truth. Interaction with angels, as we have seen from earlier accounts, is not limited to any one sense. In this chapter we

Angels

will be looking at a simple method of contact, made chiefly through intuition. I say 'chiefly' because one sense cannot be used in isolation. In order to create the right conditions for your intuition to work effectively the body and conscious mind needs to be relaxed and receptive. We will also use a visual aid in the form of word cards.

This exercise seeks to help you reawaken a primitive skill and find your own way to form a celestial relationship. This simple exercise will form the basis of all the other more specialized exercises, so it's worth spending a little time and effort at this stage. Like any other skill, it requires time, patience and practice, practice, practice. Talking with an angel is innocent, natural and comforting. How good it feels to realize that you are not alone and that there is always support and guidance on hand. All it needs is for one to ask.

Be careful for what you wish, it may come true.
Traditional Arab saying

Asking

True asking is based purely on a need to know.

Asking is not about demanding a specific item or result as this limits your request to the earthly answers you have already come up with. An answer is not always a solution, often your preferred solution will be restricted by practical circumstances and resources physical, mental or material may simply not be available to you. What would be the point of asking for divine help if you already knew the answer? Angels work through your soul. Asking is about trusting, without prejudgment and accepting the answer with faith and an open mind.

Try to hold faith, you may not recognize your answer when it comes, this does not mean you have not been answered. Be willing to listen, try not to let your ego limit you, divine guidance comes from a massive data base which is beyond our

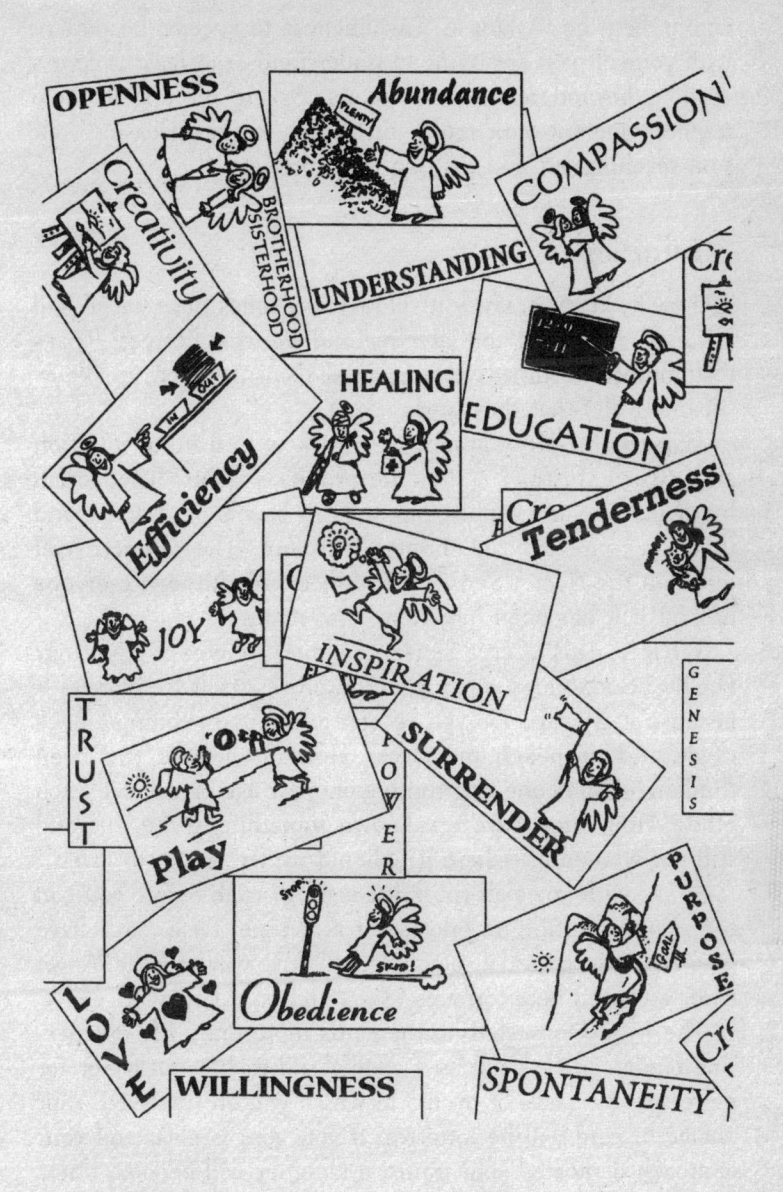

Angel calling cards

comprehension. Asking is a willingness to accept, be patient with yourself you are trying to understand or at least accept a wisdom beyond our consciousness. Asking for angelic help requires opening your mind and making space, releasing your soul reaching out and trusting your instincts.

Intuition

'I knew it, knew it, knew it!' How many times have we all had a hunch, not acted and later realized we were correct? That's your intuitive faculties working, we all recognize them and know (instinctively) that they work.

What we need to do now is learn how to use our intuition and trust it. Instinct is a subtle primitive talent. In our rush for civilization and sophistication it has become a disused, and therefore unrecognized, human attribute. The Chinese call intuition the 'Secret Sense'. Secret because although everyone has got it it has been forgotten by so many.

What is this secret sense? Memory? Seeing? Hearing? Feeling? Sometimes when intuition proves itself we dismiss it because it is scary. Do you recognize the goose bumps, neck tingle and unspoken messages? How often have you been thinking of someone and the telephone rings or you see each other? How often have you known something to be true and still not wanted to believe it? Should we try harder to listen?

So, as with any skill you must learn to walk before you can run. Concentrating on one factor at a time, flash cards have long been recognized as a simple, effective way to learn. Angel cards are used here to focus your mind on a key word.

The words suggested on the cards represent a life essence. The cards can be used as a general aid to life quality or for more specific tasks or events in which you are involved. Your choice of card will be intuitive. If your aim is clear and your approach dedicated your intuitive faculties will become finely tuned making the support you receive more powerful.

The Cards

In order to concentrate, your body and conscious mind must be relaxed and comfortable and I suggest that the cards themselves can help. They can be purchased, or making the cards can be a pleasant task. If you decide to make your own cards, you will have the advantage of a personal affinity with your cards. Also the soothing, calming process will help to put you in touch with stillness and light.

All you need is some white card (perhaps the backs of greeting cards from someone special?), scissors and coloured pencils. Yes, this is a childlike (not childish) assignment, the idea is to get in touch with feelings of innocence and simplicity. Let your mind wonder over feelings of loving and sharing without question just with faith.

Above all enjoy the process, put on a favourite jumper and have a bunch of flowers by your side, after all you are making preparations for a very special occasion. Keep it light, remember in the angelology section how angels like someone to play with. There is a Scottish saying: 'Angels can fly because they take themselves lightly'.

The Words

Find somewhere warm and light to sit where you will not be disturbed and begin by cutting your card into approx. 2 cm x 6 cm (1 inch x 3 inch) pieces. Take your time, concentrate on putting tranquillity into your task. Make approximately 55 cards or use a similar number that is special to you. Now write one word on each card representing simply the spirit, sum or substance of a pure essence. Words that can be used for meditation or, if you wish, as a mantra. Below are a few which you can add to as you become more comfortable.

Incidentally, I have it on good authority that angels can't spell! – so relax, don't spend ages thinking, let your intuition

Angels

dictate the words, make your cards attractive, a reflection of you.

Inspiration	Efficiency	Gratitude
Humour	Purpose	Integrity
Understanding	Harmony	Brother/Sisterhood
Courage	Healing	Delight
Release	Honesty	Trust
Simplicity	Birth	Grace
Clarity	Truth	Creativity
Education	Light	Strength
Love	Freedom	Power
Compassion	Openness	Flexibility
Patience	Faith	Peace
Adventure	Inspiration	Play
Transformation	Communication	
Balance	Beauty	

So now you have your own special cards to help in communing with angels, with light, with a universal mind. Next we will look at making that communication. All our basic learning was once gained through play. As with the making of the cards, the essence of this exercise is one of simplicity and enjoyment. In order to enjoy we need to be relaxed and happy, communication is always more effective if you smile.

The Place

If possible find somewhere that you can make your own special place. I hesitate to suggest out of doors, only because this should be a place you can return to time and again. A place that is, or will become, familiar and loved. If you are lucky enough to have a whole room available you can create a room of light. However, your own corner and a chair with a little table or lap tray is just fine.

Have a focal point, keep it simple, no altars please. Your focal point can be as small and modest as a house plant, a bunch of fresh flowers or maybe a special picture. Best of all, is to be near a window making your focal point something natural, constant but changing, a tree, a shrub, a plant of any kind is ideal. A plant has life and energy, it constantly regenerates, is silent and beautiful, does not demand attention but, just like an angel, what joy it gives when we take to the trouble to notice it.

Have you ever watched a cat looking for somewhere to settle? It will stalk a given area, try a couple of places and positions until it finds exactly the right spot, turn a few times to check the aspect, then flop in total relaxation. Explore the space you have until you find the right spot. Try a few different aspects, see how it feels. Give your instinct time to work, if you listen you will know where and how and, what's more, you will be happy with your choice.

Motivation

Being happy with your venue is important, also important is being happy with yourself. Physical relaxation and comfort is also important and we will spend time on that aspect. The key factor, however, is mental and emotional relaxation. Here we have a classic chicken-and-egg situation in that to be physically relaxed you must be mentally relaxed and vice versa. So let's start at the very beginning. Your relationship with yourself, which needs to be healthy and honest.

A person can be angry, frightened, grief stricken, or just plain harried and these are all valid and healthy emotions. What we sometimes forget, or get wrong, is where we place these emotions which can lead to confusion and frustration. This is where honesty comes in. Now I cannot in all honesty tell you that an angel has access to all your innermost thoughts, but I do believe that we are dealing with a vastly complex circumstance and as we said earlier an understanding that is beyond our consciousness. So common sense dictates that honesty is the best policy.

Inventory

Have you thought deeply about asking for angel support? Normally if we ask for a favour we go to friends. Normally our friends like us. Now we are going to ask an angel, who we don't yet know, to be a friend and to like us enough to proffer support and comfort. Before asking someone to like us we have to ask: Do I like myself? Have you looked that close lately? Now is a good time to make a start.

No big psychological beating of breasts, just a long clear look, what Flonda Scott Maxwell calls a Reality Inventory:

You need to claim the events of your life to make yourself yours. When you truly possess all you have been and done, which may take time, you are fierce with Reality.

Being fierce with reality requires that we break through our denial about ourselves, and our lives, layer by layer. At some point in our lives we need to stop and take a thorough inventory of who we are and what we have done. This fearless searching inventory not only focuses upon things we wish we had done in some other way, but also focuses upon our strengths and the things we have done right. So many of us forget that taking stock of ourselves means looking at what is good about us, and the things we appreciate and like about ourselves, as well as the bad things. A good idea is to make a list, one column headed positive and one negative. After all honesty is not only about mistakes it is also about the good, powerful, the creative, the loving and gentle compassionate aspects of ourselves.

When we stop and truly possess all we have been and done we are on the path to becoming who we are.

It is said that young babies can see their own angel. We have all experienced that clear direct gaze of a young child. Surely the perfect balance of wisdom and innocence. The child is simply absorbing all available information, no questions, no judgement just complete faith in the world they are experiencing at the time. This is where we are endeavouring to get to in our communication with angels. Every exercise needs to start from here.

Relaxation

Keeping the child analogy in mind, think how unconscious of its body a child is, numerous tumbles rarely result in injury because young children are naturally soft and relaxed. The child is not thinking of its body, but concentrating on what it is doing. This is the state we are looking to achieve with physical relaxation.

Before you set out on this stage may I suggest you read the next three sections through first and I will give you a recap plan at the end.

Be quiet and warm in your special place, take a time when you will not be interrupted. If you have your own method of physically relaxing so much the better. For complete beginners I would recommend sitting comfortably with one hand resting on your abdomen. Breathe deeply and feel your respirations rising and falling with your hand. Each breath brings fresh energy and life to your whole body. Focus this energy on one limb at a time. Starting with your left leg, tense your muscles, then relax and go 'soft', the same with your right leg and your trunk, arms, neck and lastly your head. Concentrate on letting your breathing admit new light and calmness into your whole body.

Angels

Meditation

Comfortably relaxed with your limbs free; no crossed legs or folded arms. Hold your cards in your hands and recall the child-like pleasure and simplicity of cutting and colouring them. Rest peacefully in your special place, let quiet music flow around you and take some time to have an 'emotional clearout'. Remember layer by layer. Above all be gentle with yourself, this is not a test, it's your personal pleasure. It's *your* angel so do it your way.

Be still, mentally and physically, think about where you are within yourself right now. Set a simple realistic goal in your mind of where you would like to move on to, one small step at a time. When you are ready gently spread out your little cards in front of you. You may be an organized person who likes to see things in neat rows all one way up, or you may prefer to see them lie at random. Do whatever feels right to you.

Your hands may be trembling a little, if you're nervous that's all right. How often have we all had an overwhelming desire to giggle at important moments in life? On a practical note, I'd say let that laugh come out and, what is more, enjoy it. I hope when you are more experienced you want to laugh aloud – out of sheer joy. Laughing through nervousness or excitement is quite natural and very understandable, here we are looking at the most natural thing in the long history of humanity, communing with our God given support system.

Contact

Reaffirm – Is your mind open and clear? Are you willing to expand awareness? Have you a genuine desire to attain your set goal? Focus your mind on the light within your mind and simply ask an angel to join you. As natural as 'will you help me please?' In time you will feel an energy or a lifting within you, a contact if you like. When beginning just let the light and

Angel Calling Cards

calm stay with you and give your instinct time and space to select one of the cards.

Welcome your angel, or the feeling you have, and give it a name. If no name presents itself, use the word on the card. Attune to the key word. Remember to say thank you! Try to visualize the essence you have instinctively chosen. If this is too difficult at first just let the word flow around you, give it energy and presence repeat it out aloud. You could find at some stage that your angel will offer you a small gift. Look out for it, it may be an image, a warmth, words in your mind, even a little shiver of joy. Whatever it is it will be natural and normal, so much so that you need experience to recognize it.

Please do not feel self-conscious about talking aloud to your angel. At first a smile and a hello is enough, just like making friends with anyone. As time drifts on the whole episode will flow along naturally, leaving you with a feeling of calm and fulfilment. Keep faith with the essence you have chosen, repeat it to yourself, let it into everyday thoughts. Let it into your dreams and gradually it will become a natural part of your consciousness. On a practical note I would suggest that you have pen and paper at hand to record your experiences. It will be helpful for you to keep track of your feelings and responses. When you wish to return to your angel, your notes will help you to focus and be aware of how you are moving along together.

The time will come, and your instinct will let you know, when it is prudent to choose another card and befriend another angel. Angels don't desert you, any more than real friends do, when you move on to discourse with another. Again, before you move on, please remember to say thank you. In time your experience and your notes will enable you to move happily amongst your celestial friends.

All this will happen if you give it time and allow for the subtleties of the contact. To illustrate may I refer you back to my own story in Chapter 2 – A beautiful creature. I note only now that I do not refer to an angel but to light and whispering

Angels

from far away. See how there was a dialogue, and the fact that the light or angel called me by name, next note – so *we* stagger ... Now my angel has joined me you see the subtle gifts I was given, guidance, cool breeze, warm sun. Whether the butterfly was an angel reincarnation or a visual gift it doesn't really matter, does it? Finally, see how the whole episode drifted to a natural end.

Recap of centring

1 Relax – mentally and physically
2 Focus – on where you are and where you want to go
3 Ask – your angel to join you, in this first exercise choose a card
4 Listen – for subtle changes in how you are thinking and feeling
5 Accept – without judgement, (even if you just feel bewildered)
6 Respond – visualize, talk to your angel, in this first exercise keep faith with your chosen essence.

Finally – let go – with gratitude.

I hope by now that it goes without saying – smile and enjoy.

The first six basic steps, known as grounding or centring, are used in all exercises so it is well worth spending time and effort here. Gradually it will become so natural you will do it without thinking. As we move through the next chapters each exercise will build upon the last. We will refer to the last exercise as 'Centring'.

Make friends with Angels, who though invisible are always with you.

St Frances de Sales 1567–1622

Finally, when you have the courage, I would like you to do a little experiment. Ask a friend if he or she believes in angels. I guarantee the first reaction will be a huge smile!

7

help for ourselves

Angel Therapy – How Does it Work?

Angel healing works in conjunction with the natural forces of our lives and bodies. The simple theory is: Physically our body cells are constantly regenerating and this is how we remain alive. Energy is created by the vibration of cells dividing and renewing. Vibration creates heat, heat creates light. At the beginning of the angelology section we saw the origins of this vibratory sequence. (Chapter 4, First Triad; Seraphim chants – the creation of life).

Seraphim – keeper of divine love. Sketch from cathedral in Cefalo, Sicily

Angelic healing takes place at a cellular level, during conversion of cells by correcting and enhancing light frequencies. Remember the constants of all the angels are light – 'shining ones' and colour, all the angels are described in radiant colours and with glowing auras. If angels are indeed intellect then the hypothesis still works, along the lines of 'thought turning to light.'

Light is created from colour, think of rainbows, so here we have the simple tools of angelic healing, light and colour. These constant energies, combined with numerous angelic characteristics: wisdom, love, compassion, patience, joy, eternal understanding, plus endless *faith* in the power of love; to name but a few, make for a powerful healing system.

The fundamental of angelic healing is based in support of our natural body functions and compassion for our spiritual well-being. We may not fully understand how angel healing works, but once you have experienced its comforts you will surely know it does. For instance, we all know how night-time terrors slide away with a warm hug. Suffering is so much more bearable with a loving hand to hold. This is what having your own angel can do for you when you feel alone.

As with any alternative therapy, and certainly with angel therapy, we return to our recipe of part fact, part folklore and part faith. In the best traditions of alternative treatments angel therapy works in co-operation with conventional physical and psychological medicine. Angels seek to share the healing process. As much as doctors cannot help unless you consult them, so angels cannot help unless you create space to receive their energy.

Energy

> *Vision is the art of seeing things invisible*
> Jonathan Swift

Bearing in mind the basic centring exercise, let's now try to reach your energy field. Settle yourself comfortably in your special place. Picture a field of light ebbing and flowing about you. Minute shining particles radiate from you and form a coloured aura around you, creating light, warmth and energy. Are you sensitive to atmosphere? Can you feel when the atmosphere is loving, tense, excited or fearful? Try then to sense the atmosphere you have already created in your special place. Listen for the small voice of your intuition giving you guidance.

The atmosphere you create contributes to the aura around you. Ether means upper air, we are now looking to locate what is called your etheric body, which is the aura or energy field around you. It has always been there. At the beginning of this book we looked at darkness being an absence. Well this is the very essence of what was meant, once you switch on to the light of your aura, energy field, etheric body, call it what you may, there will be another whole dimension to your life and spiritual powers. Your etheric body will gradually become more apparent to you and with the help of angels you can become

Help for Ourselves

aware of a profound spiritual beauty in yourself and those around you, which will make life so much more fulfiling.

Two good places to feel for your energy field are the thymus chakra and the solar plexus chakra areas. The thymus chakra is in the centre upper chest and can be located by measuring a hand's width from the bony bit as the base of your throat. The solar plexus is also centre-front body, just above your waist where the ribcage parts (see illustration of chakra centres on page 75).

Etheric exercise

To do this you need to be comfortably centred. Again, I recommend you read this section through once or twice to familiarize yourself with the actions.

First practice 'soft focusing'. Make sure your head is comfortably supported, relax your eyelids and focus on one small point just beyond your visual range until the point you are looking at becomes fuzzy. Your own sight will dictate the distance of the point you focus on. You will find as you progress through the communication exercises your eyes may naturally close, that's fine. But to start with many people find soft focusing more natural especially if you are at the stage of wanting to make notes.

Warm your hands by massage. Holding one hand with the other, place your left thumb in your right palm and rub firmly, then the other way around. Next rub the tips of your fingers on each hand together, with each stroke go further down your fingers then your palms until you are massaging your whole hands from finger tips to wrist. Begin to move your forearms rhythmically from side to side in time with your breathing. Whilst warming your hands, concentrate on clearing your mind by reaffirming (see the contact section in Chapter 6).

When your body and mind intuitively feel receptive, place your hand palm down about 15 cm (6 inches) in the upper air above the chosen chakra. Slowly move your hand towards your body and out again. Do this a few times, not looking at your hand but soft focusing. Be patient and slow and you will feel, as your palm gets closer to your body, about 10 cms (4 inches), a slight change of either heat or pressure.

When you feel this shift move your hand gently within that sphere. As you become more aware you may notice a change in your respirations or mood. As your hand encounters your energy field for the first it can be quite thrilling, a feeling of recognition perhaps? Go gently you will become more sensitive with time. As you become more confident slowly move your hand to the other chakra centre. Can you feel your hand following your etheric body? If you lose it go back, repeat the in and out stage, then try again. Remember an essential quality of angels is joy and take pleasure in your new discovery.

Remember the craze for three-dimensional pictures? The knack of how to see these pictures is available to everyone it was just a case of being let into the secret of how to do it. Some found it easier than others. Angelic communication is no parlour game, but it *is* light and cheerful, anyone can do it. Like intuition, our energy field is a natural part of our composition, we just need the skill, faith and patience to access it, like the 3-D trick.

Healing Properties

As the human and animal world has evolved, so have the angels. It is with the blessing and assistance of all the Archangels that our healing angels help us. Raphael is involved with the healing process as is the grace and wisdom of Gabriel. LaUna Huffines put it succinctly in her book *Healing Yourself with Light*: 'Angels evolve through serving the plan of evolution; they depend on human evolution for their own evolution. Their consciousness is immersed in serving humanity . . . separation from their (divine) source or resistance to higher evolution does not exist for angels. They do not withdraw from the light as humans do'.

In simple terms, what she is pointing out is that although angels have kept up with human evolution they have not lost contact with the natural gifts of nature. They carry to us the love and power of life energy. The energy from God that created all, and with it the means of nourishing and supporting that creation. The natural instinct of nature is to thrive and recreate.

Because angels cannot touch us physically they have to use more subtle means. Our hearts, our minds, our faith, our souls, in other words our very essence, is what creates the aura around us. To heal angels use their natural God given qualities which, as we have seen, include such natural attributes as light, colour and vibration, that is their aura. Because angels have always been familiar with these natural media they have the innate experience to know when a human aura or energy field is out of sync with its owner.

Each part of our body radiates energy, so the angels can reach every part to assist us to regulate, retune or reorganize the regenerative process of our body. As much as the sky and sea will produce a different colour in reaction to a particular circumstance, good and bad, so does the human body.

Angels

Colours

It is well-known that colour can affect our mood and therefore our behaviour. Stores will use bright colours to encourage us to buy, waiting areas use pastel colours to encourage us to stay calm. We all have a favourite colour, we all have a soul colour. Our soul colour is the common ground between us and the healing angels. The following simple exercise will help you to ascertain your soul colour which you can then carry with you.

Soul colour exercise

Centred happily in your special place locate your energy field as in the etheric exercise. Concentrate upon the substance of your aura, see in your mind's eye the millions of minute particles as they swirl and teem around you. Now pick up on our rainbow from earlier and let it flood your special place. Keeping your focus soft and your hand steady upon your energy field divide your rainbow into the seven colour bands.

Starting with yellow 'try on' each colour, let it flood your energy field and as it does so try to notice how you feel. What emotions come to you with each colour? Some will calm you, some will excite, some will make you feel anxious. Can you feel any reaction in your energy field, does it get warmer or colder? You may find it useful to make notes. Everything you are doing is perfectly natural, please do not think you need to be in some sort of psychic trance. Take it slowly, take a break from time to time.

As you proceed through this fascinating exercise, from yellow to orange, through the green and blue to purple you will become more attuned to the changes taking place. As you learnt to feel your energy field so you will learn to feel the ebb and flow of your reactions to the colours you are trying and begin to swop and compare. Ask your angel to help you to recognize what you feel; is it cosy or disquieting? Gradually you will find one particular colour will keep intruding. Maybe in small sparks, maybe as a gentle mist. Don't grab, but quietly gather this colour around you. Let it enter your energy field and become clear and bright.

Try to feel this colour as a liquid flowing around you, warm and soothing, bubbling and joyful as you need. Let it go to write your notes and then cuddle back again, in time leaving and finding your soul colour will be a natural process. Your soul colour is your spiritual security blanket. Use it like one, when you feel down, tired, stressed or anxious, draw your security blanket around you and feel its soft comfort healing your spirits. Whatever healing process you become involved in your soul colour will add that extra margin of comfort and security we all need at times.

Chakras

The subject of chakras is a vast one, so please accept the following as a simplistic explanation. The word *chakra* means wheel and can be compared to the wheels we met in angelology, because chakra centres convey messages from the energy field surrounding us to our mental, physical and emotional functions. In physical terms think of your aura as the 'brain' and the chakra as the nerve centres.

If you imagine the spinal column as a tree, our nerve impulses are carried by a 'branch-to-branch' system. Chakra centres radiate light using a similar method, from eight specific centres to all parts of the body. Each chakra centre has its own colour.

Angels

The chakra and the colours help you and your angel to define and direct energies to weak spots. Think of it in terms of your doctor giving you medicine for a specific malady and a tonic to aid your general health.

In angel healing terms your thymus chakra would be sending light energy to the affected area to assist regeneration of healthy cells or feelings (like the medicine) and your soul colour would support you to be positive and believe in your recovery (like the tonic for general health). The eight chakra centres, their colours and functions are illustrated for your information, however for the purposes of this book we are dealing only with the thymus chakra, which we mentioned when locating your energy field.

Thymus Chakra

Each chakra centre has three functions relating to the main areas of our daily lives; mental, physical and psychic. The thymus chakra mentally is our median for the universal brotherhood of man and for unconditional universal love and peace. Physically it covers the thymus gland, orchestrator of our immune system. The thymus gland is our natural 'defence' system and inbuilt recovery procedure if the first line of defence is overcome. In the psychic sense the thymus chakra relates to telepathy, or our unspoken relationship with others, its sense colour is aquamarine like the sea on a sunny day.

Broadly then the thymus chakra relates to the following three areas:

1 Love for ourselves and our fellow human beings.
2 Maintaining good general health physically and emotionally.
3 Our personal effect on the outside world.

As an introduction to the chakra method of angel healing let us look at getting in touch with the first of these three. This is a good general 'pick me up' when suffering from a general

Help for Ourselves

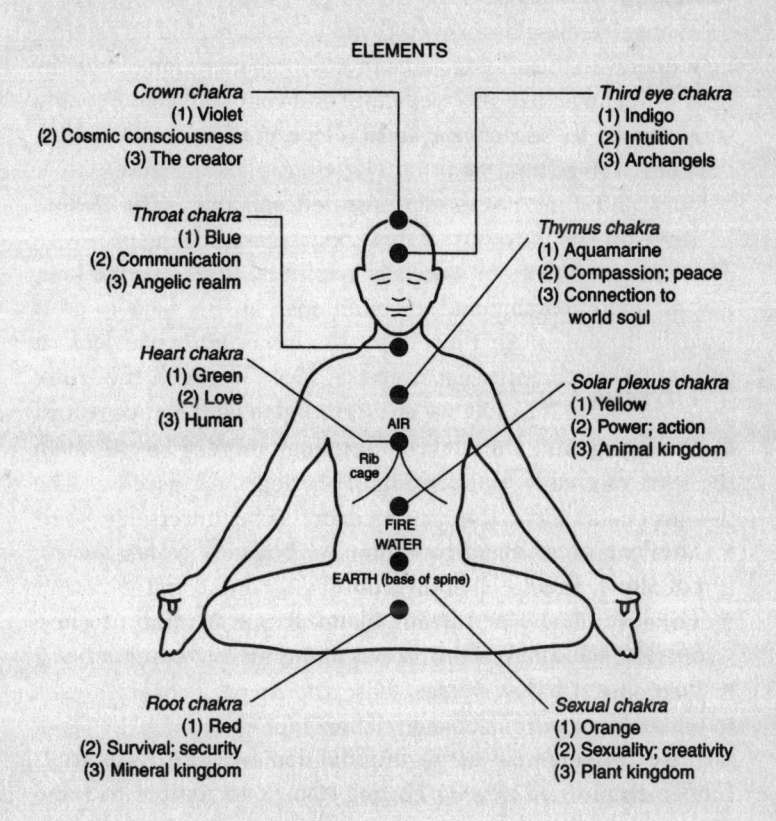

ELEMENTS

Crown chakra
(1) Violet
(2) Cosmic consciousness
(3) The creator

Third eye chakra
(1) Indigo
(2) Intuition
(3) Archangels

Throat chakra
(1) Blue
(2) Communication
(3) Angelic realm

Thymus chakra
(1) Aquamarine
(2) Compassion; peace
(3) Connection to world soul

Heart chakra
(1) Green
(2) Love
(3) Human

Solar plexus chakra
(1) Yellow
(2) Power; action
(3) Animal kingdom

AIR
Rib cage
FIRE
WATER
EARTH (base of spine)

Root chakra
(1) Red
(2) Survival; security
(3) Mineral kingdom

Sexual chakra
(1) Orange
(2) Sexuality; creativity
(3) Plant kingdom

Chakra centres of the human body

Angels

feeling of unhappiness. Sometimes it seems that, for no good reason, life is sad and grey, our soul is heavy and nothing seems worthwhile. At times like these we can all benefit from the healing powers of love.

Love

To love for the sake of being loved is human, to love for the sake of love is Angelic.

Alphonse de Lamaritine, 1790–1896

The love given to us by angels is a spiritual love, a divine love, it is all encompassing and unconditional, all you have to do is have faith and make the effort. In this exercise we look at getting in touch with that universal love. To touch the truth, the goodness and beauty we are surrounded with is the greatest of healing agents. The universal healing power of love through the thymus chakra builds up by three steps:

- The love of an angel for you – we begin to realize we are not alone, there is help available.
- The love of one person for themselves – we begin to love ourselves and have faith in our ability to live happy lives.
- Love of our fellow beings.

We use this exercise as an introduction because its basis is fundamental to all angelic healing, that is to replace bad and negative with good and positive. Have your little angel cards by you as they will come in handy later.

Universal love exercise

Good thoughts will produce good actions and bad thoughts will produce bad actions. Hatred does not cease by hatred at any time, hatred ceases by love.

Traditional Buddist saying

In this session it is important, as in all the others, to start with centring. Relax physically and be emotionally as honest as possible (reality inventory). The focus here is first to establish what is wrong, to identify the negative. To start you off here are a few suggestion of negative emotions:

- Constant criticism of self and others.
- Victimization or feeling a victim of life.
- Feelings of rejection or unworthiness.
- Fear of rejection or disappointment prohibiting action.
- Feelings of inadequacy and jealousy.
- Greed, revenge, etc. – once you get going it becomes all too easy!

You may find it useful here to write a list of the unhelpful emotions you have been experiencing. Keep it by you as you carry on to locate your thymus chakra centre, using the etheric exercise method. Remember your thymus chakra is a hands width from the base of your throat. Be aware of your breathing together with the beautiful aquamarine colour of the thymus chakra. Imagine gentle waves of aquamarine water lapping on the shores of your life. With each breath, each wave, this warm aquamarine water is reaching further into your soul.

Talk to your angel, discuss whatever is in your mind; for instance, whether you have found the right chakra

Angels

spot. Can feel light? Can feel warmth? Do not feel discouraged, if you cannot feel anything then talk to yourself, you're a nice person! If you are physically relaxed by now you will want to drop your hand. That's good, because it means you have fixed your thymus chakra in your mind and can feel the light emanating from it. Should the light wobble or fade a little, relocate the chakra centre with your hand until the light and your hand feel warm and steady again.

As you breathe to the rhythm of the beautiful aquamarine light flowing outward from your thymus chakra, replace your hand and let it move in and out to the rhythm of your breathing encouraging waves of light wider and deeper into your soul. When the ease and calmness is upon you mildly cast your eye over the negative list you made. Let each negative emotion fade into the aquamarine light, let the stress of negativity float away upon the waves lapping through your body.

Negative emotions are stifling, as they drift away on the tide enjoy the relief and lightness of heart which comes from setting your spirit free. Welcome the light, it is angelic. Within the lightness there is now room for positive supportive emotions. Now you have come to the stage of replacing negative with positive.

Have you got your angel cards by you? Use the words on the cards to inspire you; Peace; Humour; Compassion; Balance; drift on through. Let these positive powerful emotions out on to the aquamarine chakra light as it begins to dance and sparkle bringing peace and joy into your soul. Test your etheric body again, can you feel a difference? If you feel able to start writing a new list of positive healing emotions, this again is good, because it means you feel easy. However, that can wait for now as you may be feeling a little sleepy. If so, bid your angel goodbye and thanks for now, curl up into your soul colour and enjoy a refreshing rest – as contented as that cat in the sunshine.

Angel healing

As you can heal your spirit through the chakra method of light direction, so you can heal your body. However, this is another vast subject and we have already packed a lot into this chapter. Suffice it to say here that the method is the same. Light is directed in the same way to the affected area. When you feel ready to progress you will find books in Further Reading to help you in more detail. This book is meant to be a guide to give you the general idea of angels in our lives and to get your started. However, for general debilitation and recovery, I suggest the universal love exercise will be a great help.

We have covered briefly the essence of angelic help and healing. Identify what is bad, identify what is good and replace the former with the latter. Sounds simple, but aren't all the best ideas simple? The love exercise incorporated everything we have discussed thus far and is indeed a tall order for a beginner. If you have reached this stage with anything more than a rueful smile then congratulations.

Talking with angels is like making love, you can't force it. When the time is right, your mind and body receptive, it will happen and it will be wonderful. To achieve results takes time, practice and faith. Please be patient with yourself and your angel will give you endless help.

There are rooms of experience that some of us have not yet entered.

John Steinbeck

Angels

Knowing where the rooms are and how to switch on the light is a good start.

8

help for others

When we pray for someone an angel goes to sit on their shoulder. Having concentrated up to now on an individual relationship with our angels we try expanding our capacity to share celestial knowledge and beauty. The basis of all good communication is watching, listening and caring and this is, after all, how angels communicate with us. In relationships angels can help by showing fresh insight; we look for assistance from Gabriel the angel of grace and wisdom. We will stay with the thymus chakra; its third function is assistance with telepathy or our affect on others.

Watching – Young Children

Native peoples of the Canadian central Arctic still hold that a baby is born accompanied by its own guardian angel. The baby is given the name of a recently deceased elderly family member

Angels

and is revered and respected with great tolerance. It is not until the child has begun to acquire its own personality that the parents choose a 'given' name. This is usually when the child is about five years old.

At this stage we understand that the baby's birth guardian angel retreats to give control to the parents. This is borne out by a story I heard from young parents with a five year old and a new baby who were relaxing quietly one evening when they heard a little voice through the loud speaker of their baby alarm.

'Hello baby sister, I can't go to sleep 'cos I keep on thinking'. Silence. 'Better not go down for a drink of water, they'll send me back 'cos they don't know what I'm thinking in my head.' Then a very rushed little voice 'Baby can you tell me about the angels? 'Cos I forget 'cos I've got to keep remembering to say thank you and share my toys and things.'

Kerubim – keepers of wisdom. Sketch from cathedral in Cefalo, Sicily

Help for Others

How does the famous prayer go? 'Out of the mouths of babes and sucklings hast thou ordained strength . . .' We must treasure our children and watch and learn from them for they are in the presence of angels.

Watching – Social

We all like people watching. I have to confess it is a favourite holiday pastime of mine. Holidays are about having time off; try also to plan small amounts of 'time off' into your everyday life. The next project I'm going to suggest is modest and everyday, but one I think few of us actually set out to accomplish and monitor. Earlier I suggested that you ask someone if they believe in angels and watch their reaction. This is the same idea but much simpler.

To make this more successful I'll give you a hint of a little cheat. Pick a bright sunny day, when you are feeling good, maybe after an angel card experience. Take your angel with you. Put an angel card in your pocket; perhaps Openness, Delight, Humour or Joy. Quietly locate your thymus chakra and try to carry its aquamarine light in your spirit. In time it will become second nature to you to realize you are not setting out on any of life's paths alone when you have accepted angels into your life. Can you share a little of that joy? I think so.

Take yourself and your new found awareness into a public place. Anywhere where there are likely to be a few people, such as a town centre, park, supermarket or department store. Watch the people. How many of them have got their heads down, how many of them are smiling, with their bodies as well as their faces? Wait for the right opportunity, (trust your instinct) it will be fleeting and ordinary, walking toward someone on the pavement, standing in a queue, parking the car. Make steady eye contact and smile, so you both know who your smile is for.

Just that, make eye contact and smile at seven different people. I have done this, some said hello, some looked a little startled, and all but one smiled back (you can't win them all). What I learnt was that people do respond if you reach out, what is more I felt good and I do believe my 'victims' responded to my modest rays of smiling light. Try it.

Listening – Sensory

Listening is not only hearing but watching too. We are all familiar with the observation, I knew something was up the moment they walked into the room. It is known as sensory listening. Sensory listening is a skill that you can learn from your experience with angel communication. Remember the 'energy' section? When you are aware of your own aura you can become aware of the aura of others.

The angels trumpet their joy when it is shared by many.

Examples of aura are around us all the time. Have you ever read a story to a group of children? Once you have caught the imagination of one, they will all begin to concentrate, you can feel the aura, the atmosphere of concentration and enjoyment. At a celebration, a party, there is an atmosphere of happiness, people happy in the company of others for a common enjoyment.

Take it even wider, think of a sporting event. It is well known that sportsmen are sensitive to the atmosphere of the crowd. Watch and feel as people leave an event that has been good and successful. The atmosphere crackles, everyone is happy. We go home with a lovely feeling of contentment because it has been a shared experience.

The action is best which produces the greatest happiness for the greatest number.

Francis Hutcheson, 1694–1746

Listening – Hearing

To listen properly is a completely unselfish unselfconscious gift. You must be wholly concentrated on what you are listening to, no judgement, no preconception of a solution. This is why angels will always hear us because their whole desire is for our peace and contentment, not their own, they already have peace and that is why they are such good listeners. To really listen is the most valuable gift you can give to others, so it is worth spending time honing such a skill, for skill it certainly is, and one that can be learned. Most of us love to talk, but how many of us love to listen?

Music – listening exercise

Most of us love to listen to music and it is a good medium through which to become aware of listening skills. Make your own choice of music, choose carefully, it should be of at least 10 minutes duration. As you centre yourself in preparation you may care to invite an angel of Israfel the Angel of Music to accompany you in this exercise. Do not start the music until you are happy that your mind is clear and focused, you need to be listening to the sound of this music not to any preconceived emotions you have attached to it. Real listening is like the angels, non-judgemental.

When you do start the music, let it fill your special place, enjoy it, share it with your angel. Tell your angel about the music, what it is; for example, jazz, folk, classical, its title, the instruments, the performers. In other words know what you are listening to. Now be quiet, no more talking. Listen now beyond the general to the particular. There will be more than one voice, more than one sound.

Angels

Distinguish the lead voice or instrument from the accompaniment. Try distinguishing the instruments and listen to one at a time. Listen harder, hear the different phrases, the pauses, the repeats. Try to identify a common phrase or melody and notice when it is repeated. If you are listening to a ballad or folk song hear the words, do they tell a story? Is there a repeated chorus? Is the chorus trying to impress something on the listener? If you are listening to an orchestral piece, what is the music saying to you? What is its message? You are more likely to know this if, as we said, you know what you are listening to. When the music has finished continue to sit quietly with your angel. Listen to the silence. Is it really silence? Turn on again to the sounds around you. What can you hear? Neighbours or cars, someone else in the house, wind in the trees, electrical static from the music centre? How much we hear without paying attention to what we are hearing.

Listening – caring

Unbosom yourself, said Wimsey. Trouble shared is trouble halved.
                                        Dorothy L. Sayers 1893–1957

A person in trouble is unlikely to turn to someone they sense is afraid or uncaring. A smiling face hiding a despairing heart is a lethal combination. Please bear this in mind when you set out to take angel assistance to another, not only for them but yourself. Before you offer help, be humble enough to ask for help for yourself. This is not selfish it is practical common sense. Remember you are not alone, ask your angel for support and guidance and it will come.

There will, of course, be occasions when there is no space

Help for Others

for long leisurely centring exercises. Angels are aware of emergencies, think back to the tractor incident at Lee Abbey. I am quite sure that one of the monks noticed what was happening and sent up a rapid prayer. An honest heartful 'Please I need some help here' from an open soul will not go unanswered.

To listen with care is the most valuable healing you can give to another. The angels look for no reward other than our faith, so we must suspend all personal emotion when listening to someone in pain. Remember '. . . to love for the sake of love is angelic'. Curative listening involves all the social, sensory and hearing skills we have already discussed.

Watch the body language, from a distressed person these will include; tightly folded arms, crossed legs, hunched shoulders, rigidity, clasped hands or, in extreme cases, a foetal position. Recall the pivotal role relaxation plays in chakra healing and encourage this in your friend by being relaxed yourself.

People will often 'mirror' behaviour, as we try to mirror the calm and serenity of our special angels. Try to establish eye contact, adjust your own body language to a listening posture. Legs beside each other, body slightly inclined towards your friend, head slightly to one side, arms apart with your hands open. Although your friend may not actually see it, he or she will feel it and it will also allow your etheric body freedom to transmit chakra light and calm. Your own chakra energy can transmit powerful support and encouragement.

A popular misconception is that one should 'encourage' people to talk by asking questions. Direct questions will only serve to distract a person from what they want to say. Angels do not ask questions, they wait for us to find our own way. Forget the how, what, when, where scenario. A gentle 'tell me'; positive body light and assurance that there is plenty of time is enough. Then wait – quietly.

Angels

> *The surest way to lose a friend is to tell him something for his own good.*
>
> Sid Ascher

Although we all like to give advice, bear in mind that initial angel communication section on asking in Chapter 6. Whatever is given, it is up to us to interpret and use the support *positively*. Well, as discussed in my introduction to Chapter 1 . . . There always is always a negative to consider. So whatever opinions you decide to pass on, remember that once you have made your suggestions there is nothing you can do about how your wisdom may be used or construed. There is a great deal of sense in the observation that silence is golden. Angels are golden.

Sharing A Centring Experience

> *Grief can take care of itself, but to get the full value of joy, you must have someone to divide it with.*
>
> Mark Twain 1835–1910

So far in this chapter we have looked at using one's own light and chakra energy to help a third party. However, if that third party is willing to co-operate and you can work together, the supportive energies will be much more powerful and healing for you both. For telepathy to work successfully between two people you need to first to share the basic centring exercises in Chapter 7.

I would suggest a good way to bring this about is by making a tape recording of the first five basic steps; relaxation; motivation; inventory; meditation and contact. Like the making of angel cards, the actual creation of such a tape can be a beneficial shared learning experience. You may well have different reality inventories; however, making clear understandable declarations to another can be enlightening. The real value of centring

Help for Others

with another is that it is such good practice, it requires great patience and faith in each other's acceptance. The basis for all successful angelic communication.

Telepathy

Telepathy is like intuition and I believe that it is a basic attribute we are all born with. Like any skill, music, sports, languages, if you do not develop your talent it will remain dormant, but nevertheless an integral part of the person. I suggest that if you and your partner have shared a meaningful centring experience you will have already experienced the fundamentals of telepathy; i.e. recognition; understanding and empathy.

Please don't make a heavy session out of this procedure, take a break, play some music, move around, share a smile and a hug. After your mutual centring, compare notes and, I think, on more than one occasion you will find that you both have experienced that feeling of 'been there, done that, got the tee shirt' . . . Remember why angels can fly?

Chakra alignment exercise

It can in no sense be said that heaven is outside of anyone – it is within

Emanual Swedenborg, Swedish scientist,
writer and philosopher

When you have both happily completed the centring exercises and are ready, have pen and paper to hand and sit facing each other about 30 cm (12 inches) apart. Firstly, locate your own energy field as we did in the Etheric exercise in Chapter 7. Next, maintaining steady eye contact try to locate your partner's energy field. You will

Angels

need to help each other as distances and feel will vary with each individual. Don't spend too long on this, 10 minutes each is quite enough. However, as we said earlier if one of you feels a self-conscious giggle coming on, let it out, that's natural. You are supposed to be enjoying this. Now take turns to stand one behind the other and locate your partner's thymus chakra. Use only one hand and keep the other away from any contact with either body. Recall the beautiful aquamarine colour, feel the gentle waves emanating from this centre. Close your eyes and let your intuition take over, let your soul reach out to the energies coming from this other person, count your inhalations and exhalations together and try to establish a rhythm between you.

As the light flows it will form a triangle between you, your angel and your partner. This love can become a great healing agent. It can support you both in gaining freedom. Freedom from anxiety, willingness to overlook weakness, reverence for the brotherhood of man and great joy. The love you can both experience is akin to the love of angels. The love you can experience here transcends romantic or family love, which focuses on the personal, rather it centres upon spiritual love. Spiritual love is like the sunshine and the rain, it brings light and life to us all regardless of religion or status. The love you can both exchange gives each of you the freedom to be yourselves with a personality which is growing and evolving in the presence of angels upon the soothing healing light of the aquamarine thymus chakra.

Once again I say, limit the time you spend doing this, especially at first, as we said before let the experience drift naturally to its conclusion. However, please remember to bid your angel goodbye with gratitude. When you have given each other some space, had a drink and a stretch, make your notes individually and then, an important part of this particular exercise, compare notes. Sharing your experiences will heighten the encounter. It will make what happened more alive and vital to you both. What did you visualize? Did you chance upon the same images and feelings? Did you detect any blockages that you can work upon in the future? Some common angelic manifestations can be gathered from our earlier stories. A third voice telling you something. A sweet or familiar smell is common. Warmth or tingling down the back of the neck, laughter or even tears. Did the angels send a little gift? Did you feel a special calm or joy? Treasure these small gifts and share them.

Healing a Relationship

Sooner or later you've heard about all your best friends have to say. Then comes the tolerance of real love

Ned Rorem, American writer

We know we really should not have done or said what we did and sorry does not seem enough. We are human, we have all done it. The love we truly feel seems sullied, what can we do? This last exercise will put you in touch with universal love, as given to us by angels, and help you to encompass it in your own life and perhaps that of others.

Universal love exercise

As with all the other exercises this one builds on what we have already discussed. Before you start I find it helps in this instance to have two 'things'. One to represent yourself and one to represent the other person involved. Two lighted candles would be good, two flowers perhaps. Personally I have two pieces of moonstone that I hold in my hands. The choice as always is yours, whatever feels natural and comfortable. Wrap yourself in your soul colour and connect with your angel who will understand that your soul is sore.

If you are using stones, caress one stone in your hand; if you are using a flower focus upon it. Visualize the person you have hurt. Ask your angel to help you do an honest reality inventory on the other person as you concentrate on the object that represents this other person. Do not reject anything however small or silly. Then take the second object that represents you. Spell out the hurt to your angel without judgement. When all is spelt out honestly, locate your thymus chakra and let the aquamarine light connect the triangle as you did in the previous exercises. Experience once again that universal spiritual love.

Ask your angel what you need to do to heal the hurt between you. The answer will come floating in on the waves of light. Give it time and accept, no preconditions. Gently bring both objects together, in your sight or in your hands and they will form their own light and calm. This, although you may not know it at the time, is your solution. What you have received is the gift of grace which will enable you to solve the problem between you; your conscience and, thus, between you and the person you have hurt.

This is a lovely exercise which, with a little adjustment, can be used to connect you with loved ones who are away from you and may need support. Angels do not have our concept of time and distance so I simply hold my stones and ask my angel to show me how to close the gap. In my experience it brings great comfort and closeness to my loved ones.

What have we Learnt?

What do you think such exercises as these purport to teach us? One thing is clear, we are given the choice between a positive or negative attitude. We strive for freedom within a secure faith in the divinity of life. If we go back to our reality inventory, what is here and now is real. The present I believe is a present from the angels. Put down the past and do not lust for the future. Life is this moment do not waste it. It will not come again. Watch the light *now* and enjoy this gift of the present as we did in the innocence of our childhood when we were unwittingly in the presence of angels.

Conclusion

> *Angels – They are the first and most excellent creation*
> B. Herber-Harcch, Zoe cleric

It is not the intention of this book to prove that angels exist, rather to provide the pathways to enable readers to undertake a personal search for their own evidence of angels.

I believe angels are all around us, whether we believe or how we believe is highly personal. The purpose of the book is to show ways of finding angels through normal natural channels like love and understanding. Is the resurgence of interest in angels part of our evolution? Are we moving towards a greater understanding of our destiny?

So to return to our opening question: What is an angel?

Angels

Anthony Gormley, who produced the magnificent *Angel of the North* sculpture reckons:

> *Nobody's ever seen an angel which is why we have to keep imagining them.*

Do you know any different?

further reading and resources

General

A Book of Angels – Sophy Burnham, Rider, London

Ask Your Angels – Alma Daniel, Timothy Wyllie and Andrew Ramer, Judy Paitkus, London

Angel at my Shoulder – Glennyce S. Eckersley, Rider, London

Angels: Lifting the Veil – Thomas Keller and Deborah Taylor, Hampton Roads Co, USA

Angelology

Angels – Peter Lamborn Wilson, Thames and Hudson, London

Angels: An Endangered Species, Malcolm Godwin, Boxtree, London

Healing

Healing Yourself with Light – LaUna Huffins, H.J. Kramer Inc, Tiburon, California

Your Healing Power – Jack Angelo, Judy Piatkus, London

Angels

Chakras

Chakras – Naomi Ozaniec, Hodder & Stoughton, London

The Chakras – C.W. Leadbetter, Theosophical, London

Feng Shui

Feng Shui – Richard Craze, Hodder & Stoughton, London

Background

Knowledge of Angels – Jill Paton Walsh, QPD with Colt Books, London

Angel Cards

Music Designs Inc., 4650 North Port Washington Road, Milwaukee, WI 53212–1062, USA
(Available in several languages)